Endorsements

Tools for Effective Parenting, by Dr. Parnell Donahue, spotlights the important role parents play in the lives of their children, e. g. **Our Children are listening** ... Your teen may roll their eyes and act as though they are tuning you out but they are NOT.... They listen and watch your every move.

This book teaches that respect plays a huge part in guiding a child from infancy through their teenage years and into adulthood. Dr. Par teaches that children who are respected and loved have a better chance of navigating the waters of the teenage years and that respect cultivates the much yearned for trust in their parents. Dr. Par's message to us parents is that children are to be respected and reminded they are loved very much.

Dr. Par brings much credibility to his work. He's a Pediatrician, Father, and Grandfather. All of which helps me appreciate his thought provoking ideas and support for me as a parent. His background provides both a common sense approach and a medical foundation for the best way of dealing with many parent/child issues, especially those facing teens. I also appreciated

Dr. Par's ability to be direct and clear with advice that would be helpful for any parent or care giver.

I found his previous book, *Messengers in Denim,* tremendously helpful in preparing my husband and me for the teen years just ahead. Our child is still young, but will be a teen too soon! Both books stress how creating a nurturing environment at home involves what we choose to do outside as well as inside our homes.

Dr. Par's stories and examples have taught me that I am not alone; there are many parents with questions and challenges just like mine, and he is there to help us cope and shape our kids' character. The decisions we make day to day profoundly affect our lives and the lives of our family. I valued most the validation I got when I read his thoughts on the importance of family dinners and his firmness on NO Electronic devices at the family dinner table, NO TV in the bedroom and even his lessons on teen dating in High School.

I highly recommend, *Tools for Effective Parenting,* to every parent or care giver, whether you are a new parent or in the midst of the teen years. There is much to learn and Dr. Par's professional and practical advice helps us along the way.

Anne Holtz
Glenshaw, Pennsylvania

It's been stated that parenting can be a long and often lonely road especially on those days when you're absolutely certain that no parent has ever gone through what you're going through. *Tools for Effective Parenting* is a very effective place to turn to as a resource and a "go to" guide where you'll find support, humor and comfort, often best described through personal stories by the children themselves.

It doesn't preach. Instead, it reminds us, gently, of what we, as parents must learn to do: namely, listen, listen and listen to our children. Dr. Donahue's sense of compassion both as a pediatric medical specialist and father is clearly evident throughout the book.

It is packed with such timeless nuggets of information regarding peer pressure, organized religion, dinner as a family, and many more topics, each with a great message summarized by helpful tips!

As a health professional, and a new parent, I am honored to write about this book. And I believe that my child's experiences will be filled with more joy, wonder and fulfillment, as he grows up rich in the solid values and beliefs that Dr. Donahue has written about.

Gary M. Klein, MD, MPH
Charlotte, North Carolina.

tools FOR Effective Parenting

tools FOR Effective Parenting

Parenting With Dr. Par

PARNELL DONAHUE, M.D.

TATE PUBLISHING
AND ENTERPRISES, LLC

Published by Tate Publishing & Enterprises, LLC
127 E. Trade Center Terrace | Mustang, Oklahoma 73064 USA
1.888.361.9473 | www.tatepublishing.com

Tate Publishing is committed to excellence in the publishing industry. The company reflects the philosophy established by the founders, based on Psalm 68:11,
"The Lord gave the word and great was the company of those who published it."

Cover design by Rhezette Fiel
Interior design by Jake Muelle

Published in the United States of America

ISBN: 978-1-62563-690-4
1. Family & Relationships / Child Development
2. Family & Relationships / Ethics & Morals
13.08.19

Other books by Parnell Donahue

Germs Make Me Sick, *a Health Handbook for Kids*

Sports Doc, *Medical Advice, Diet, Fitness Tips, and Other Essential Hints for Young Athletes*

Messengers in Denim, *the Amazing Things Parents Can Learn from Teens*

My Prayer for You

Fathering four children has been the highlight of my life. When I look back at the things I have done, every accomplishment pales compared to the pride I have in these four young adults. I never imagined parenting could be so much fun and so rewarding. My prayer is that *Tools for Effective Parenting* will help you have an equally wonderful experience as a parent. God bless you all!`

Dedication

I am honored to dedicate this book to the hard working parents of today's children. These men and women are always an inspiration to me. To their kids they are an inspiration, as well as supporters, protectors, comforters, teachers and role models.

We often hear, "Our future lies in the hands of our children", but in truth it does not. It lies in the hands of their parents. To them, this work is humbly dedicated.

Foreword

When I was growing up and there were medical questions, every parent consulted Dr. Spock. Not to be confused with the Vulcan of Star Trek fame, Dr. Benjamin Spock was a pediatrician who wrote *The Common Sense Book of Baby and Child Care,* in 1946. This book influenced parenting for generations and in its first 52 years sold more copies than any book except the Bible. It was, in many ways, every parent's bible for child rearing[1]. It changed the way parents nurtured and interacted with their young children, encouraging them to treat their children as individuals[2]. Dr. Spock's message to parents was "**You know more than you think you do**".

Fourteen years after Dr. Spock graduated from Columbia University's College of Physician and Surgeons, Dr. T. Berry Brazelton, another noteworthy pediatrician, graduated from the same institution. He followed a path similar to Dr. Spock's and spent his life learning and teaching about the psychological development of babies and children[3]. His television series "What Every Baby Knows" aired on Lifetime from 1983-1995 and provided a platform for this soft-spoken pediatrician to share advice on strengthening families. [4] I remember watching "What Every Baby Knows" as a teen and, although not particularly taken with the content of the program at the time, Dr.

Brazelton's quiet but confident way made an impression that has lingered throughout my life. He believed that **"Your baby knows more than you think he does."**

Recently I was part of a team of doctors presenting an educational program for other physicians and behavioral health experts. The focus of the workshop was to raise the confidence and skill level of those of us who work with youth on a regular basis; during this presentation I had the pleasure of working with Dr. Parnell Donahue. He struck me, at first, as being perhaps the most senior physician in the room and I wondered why he would want to spend a beautiful Saturday morning in a lecture. It didn't take long, however, for Dr. Donahue's passion for working with youth to become apparent. During a role-play portion of the workshop Dr. Donahue demonstrated his approach to speaking with troubled teens. I, as one of the faculty teaching HIM, was captivated by his calmness, his compassion, and his ability to speak with a young patient in a way that would result in complete trust and confidence in him. It was beautiful! It's a skill that comes from the art of medicine, rather than its science.

Not having met Dr. Donahue previously I did what any modern-day pediatrician would do during the next break in the workshop: I Googled him! There I found the brief history of Dr. Parnell Donahue—a pediatrician in practice for many years who has built his practice around treating children, especially adolescent, as individuals. Armed with this information and unfair advantage I approached Dr. Donahue at the end of the seminar and introduced myself. As fate would have it, I quickly learned that Dr. Donahue was the father of two physicians with whom I have worked and whom I greatly respect: Dr. Sean Donahue, a renowned professor of pediatric ophthalmologist at Vanderbilt, and Dr. Brian Donahue, associate professor of pediatric cardiac anesthesiology also at Vanderbilt Medical Center. There's a lot to be gleaned about a man from knowing his adult children and it was obvious to me that this gentle man before me was a man of integrity.

As Dr. Spock and Dr. Brazelton before him, Dr. Donahue's passion is in connecting with his patients and helping to strengthen their families. However, Dr. Donahue's focus is on what is arguably the most difficult population of patients— adolescents. Through his candid exchanges with teens and young adults Dr. Donahue has been able to influence generations of young people and assist their parents in coping with, and actually participating in, the development of their teens through their transition to adulthood.

Dr. Donahue's years of experience and countless conversations with parents, adolescent patients, and patients of all ages, makes *Tools for Effective Parenting*, a roadmap for parents as they lead their children from infancy through childhood and into adulthood to become people of character. It is especially useful as parents and their kids navigate the challenging teen age years. Learn the lessons told through his patient's stories and his experience. Listen to your children. Spend time with them. Set clear expectations and, perhaps most importantly, lead by example. Deep down it's what every adolescent already knows. **Your kids know more than you think they do**.

Michelle D. Fiscus, MD, FAAP
President-Elect, Tennessee Chapter of the
American Academy of Pediatrics

1 Jane E. Brody, Final Advice From Dr. Spock: Eat Only All Your Vegetables, The New York Times, June 20, 1998, accessed May 18, 2012.

2 Dr. Spock's Baby and Child Care at 65

3 http://www.brazelton-institute.com/berrybio.html

4 http://www.imdb.com/title/tt1062860/releaseinfo?ref_=tt_dt_dt

Acknowledgments

I wish to thank my son Rafe who was my library research worker and helped with my word processor and computer. I owe him a big thank you.

I also need to thank MapleTree Publishing editors Rachel Terry, Larisa White Reyes, and Gail Howick who gave much-needed support and helpful suggestions as well as excellent critique when I wrote *Messengers in Denim* from which much of this book is taken. Thank you, Rachel, Laurisa, and Gail! Thanks too, to Shawn Collins, Travis King, book designer Jake Muelle and cover designer Rhezette Fiel from Tate Publishing.

A special thanks to my wife Mary and our four kids. Without them, this book could not have been written. Today these kids all have their Ph.D.s, two are also M.D.s; all are highly successful professionals. They have shared with us fourteen grandkids. We are so grateful.

I must also give a great big thank you to the thousands of parents and the kids whom I have known over the years, especially those kids who shared the stories mentioned in this book. These parents and their kids taught me about children, teenagers, parenting, and life in general.

A final word of gratitude to all them for trusting me to serve the medical needs of their children; they have been a blessing.

Table of Contents

Part IV: Habits

Part V: Economics

Introduction

Some years ago I attended a workshop where Brother Booker Ashe was the keynote speaker. His lecture was punctuated with multiple, powerful stories; stories of people, events, and ideas. These stories took us from tears to laughter and back again. He ended with cheers and the applause of a standing ovation. It was apparent that he had studied drama and used it to make his point.

When I had a chance to talk with him I asked his permission to use some of his stories in my work. Here is his reply:

> "Use anything I said if it can help someone. And you don't need to quote me. These are not my stories; they are stories of God's people. They are God's stories, or maybe I should say they are everybody's stories. You know, Brother," he went on, "there are no new stories, just old recycled stories, just like there are no new ideas and no new wisdom. Everything I said has been said before and will be said again, either by you or by somebody else … most likely both. So, don't worry about who said it first. Learn from it if you can; and remember, everybody learns from everybody else."

I love stories! We all have a story. In 1989 Robert Coles, a pediatric psychoanalyst wrote *The Call of Stories.* Twenty-four years later it still sells well. In it he says stories contain wisdom that guides us throughout life. Stories both instruct and entertain and they are the best teachers because they are so easy to remember. The Bible, another book of stories, has been around for thousands of years and has been a best seller for centuries. Most of the Old Testament and all most all of the New are stories, and after all these years–actually centuries–we are still learning from them.

Although not on the caliber of The Bible, *Tools for Effective Parenting* is a collection of stories told to me by kids in my years of pediatric practice. Hidden in these stories are parenting lessons; from them came the tools you will read about in this book.

Like the stories, and the kids who told them, these tools are the ordinary things we see every day but often overlook their importance. Family, Religion, Peers, Attitude, and Economics aren't usually looked at as tools. But in truth they are nothing less. You will see how these kids' stories will help you become a more effective parent.

Because *Tools for Effective Parenting* is not a **how to** parent book, but a **how to be a** parent book, it is different from most other parenting books. It avoids the situational approach which many parenting experts use in their books. These situational parenting books state problems or situations that a parent might face and discuss ways to handle them. No book can contain all or even most of these situations. Instead *Tools* offers a principled approach to parenting. Be aware of these principles, and parenting will become easier because it is more effective.

In essence, this is a book about ordinary kids teaching extraordinary lessons. The stories are all true, though I have changed many of the circumstances and used fictitious names to protect patient confidentiality.

I have included "Parenting Tips" at the end of each section that summarize the parenting concepts discussed.

Most of the teenagers referenced in this book listened to their parents and learned to respect them, their judgment, their values, and their way of life. Through them we learn the qualities their parents possessed that made it possible for them to raise emotionally, mentally, and physically healthy children.

As you turn these pages, be prepared to meet some kids who will entertain, excite, amaze, and enlighten you, just as they did me. And if you listen—really listen—to the kids you know, you, too, will hear many words of wisdom that will help you design a parenting style capable of producing a much needed product in today's world: honest, well-balanced, hard-working young men and women of character. Learn from them, and take pride in knowing that by applying the principles taught by the kids in this book, your kids can be just as capable and wonderful as those who related these stories to me.

Part I

Home Life

As much as it might scare you, your children mirror you. They reflect your opinions and values. They are becoming you! And that's how it should be.

In this section you will meet some ordinary teenagers who realize that the values needed to become outstanding, successful individuals are taught by parents. And you will recognize that parenting is not a technique; it is a way of life. It is digging into the depths of your soul to find the character to transmit integrity, moral strength, and leadership to your children. This is easy if we parents emulate these qualities ourselves, but without them, good parenting is impossible. Young people—teens especially—have acute noses for hypocrisy and abhor the insincere. On the other hand, they are drawn to leaders who practice what they preach … and good parents are "leaders" in the truest sense of the word.

Tool 1

Listen

A wise son heareth his father, but a scorner heareth not rebuke.

—Proverbs 13:1

Talking with kids is always the most exciting part of any health evaluation and also the most educational—if not for the patient, at least for me. I learn so much by talking and listening to kids of any age, but especially teenagers. The American Medical Association believes that talking with and listening to teens is the most important part of a teenager's health evaluation. I would add that talking with and listening to kids is the most important part of parenting. For in listening we hear, and in hearing we show them how to listen to us.

Luke is a case in point. He was in for an annual health evaluation (which he described as number 75, although he was only 16). He jokingly complained that his mother was always "dragging him in for another physical." I had never met his construction worker dad, but I was soon to learn something about his character.

"Do you smoke cigarettes?" I asked, already knowing what Luke's answer would be.

"Never, not a chance," Luke responded. But then anticipating many of the next questions he said, "My dad would kill me if I ever smoked, drank, or had sex!"

"Your dad would kill you?"

"Oh, no, no," Luke clarified. "He would never ever kill me; but I think it would probably kill him! He's been around a long time and has seen a lot of bad stuff happen, so he knows what's best. And he lets me know what's right and what's not. I can't imagine facing my dad with tobacco or alcohol on my breath, or worse yet, having to tell him I got some girl pregnant or had an STD. If I let him down, I don't know if we could get through it. I guess it's sort of like *dad knows best, so listen to him.*"

"Luke," I responded, "that was a whole lesson in parenting. Know where you stand and let your kids know, then love them enough that they would not want to disappoint you by doing the wrong thing. Thanks for making it so simple. I'll have to have you talk to some of my parent groups," I kidded.

"Thanks," he blushed. "But it's true."

"Do you think you're unique in what you just said, or do other kids think like that, too?"

"Do you mean, 'Do other kids smoke, drink, do drugs, or have sex?' or 'Do other kids listen to their parents?'"

"I know the answer to the first question, but what about the second one?" I asked.

"Pretty much, kids do what their parents do or what their parents expect them to do. I know some kids whose dads gave them condoms. To me that says, 'Go ahead, have sex.' But that's not what my dad says. I have a girlfriend and sure, we'd like to have sex. But no way am I going to go against what Dad says, not in this life!"

"I sure would like to meet your dad," I said. "He must be some kind of a guy."

"He sure is. He played football for the University of Kentucky. I'd like to play there, too. Dad always works during the day so he can't come in here, but if you come to any of our home games, I'll make sure you get a chance to meet him."

"I'll do that," I promised.

Later, I did; and Luke's dad was as impressive as Luke. I also had a chance to meet Luke's brothers in the following years, and they all had the same attitude. Apples don't fall far from the tree.

Too many parents today think they have no influence on their kids' beliefs and behavior, yet every study I've read (and there are many of them) shows that kids respect and listen to their parents.

In the 2005 Horatio Alger survey on The State of Our Nation's Youth, [1] 68 percent of the girls ages 14 to 19 and 70 percent of boys that age named a parent, sibling, or other family member as their role model. Only 15 percent named a friend, and even fewer mentioned an entertainment celebrity or an athlete.

To test these national statistics, I asked the 103 teens I evaluated one summer, who most influenced their values of right and wrong. Of these, 83 said mom, dad, or parents; three said brothers or sisters; three credited themselves as their main influence; three said others (teachers, coaches, ministers); while three had no one to credit. Only eight said friends. (One 15-year-old boy actually said Rush Limbaugh.) Like it or not, parents everywhere are the main role models for their children.

Not only do parents have a major role in influencing values, their expectations also greatly influence future performance. A study conducted by the University of Minnesota[2] on 12,000 kids in grades seven through twelve concluded: "If parents expect adolescents to get good grades and refrain from sex, those expectations influence the adolescents' behavior powerfully through twelfth grade, regardless of family income, race, or single- or dual-parent status." The lead researcher, Dr. Michael Resnick, said, "Adolescents are often very effective at convincing us that what we say is irrelevant to their lives, and the mistake we make as adults is that we believe it."

The study further indicated that "the more teenagers felt loved by their parents the less likely they were to abuse drugs or alcohol, smoke, have sex, or commit violence or suicide."

It's clear that kids adopt their parents' values. To clarify these values for their children, parents must let their kids know where they stand and why. This doesn't call for a lecture, which would most likely force the kids to hold their hands over their ears, physically as well as metaphorically; instead, parents should do as Luke's dad did, and tell of the times he saw "bad stuff happen," why it happened, its consequences, and how it might have been avoided.

These teaching moments happen all the time: when we see someone drinking too much at a ball game; when we see inappropriate displays of affection in public; when we see scantily dressed adults; when we read about an outburst of anger leading to a shooting; and when news stories tell us about drug busts, lung cancer, teen pregnancy, AIDS, and other STDs. Unfortunately, the opportunities are countless.

Our instinct is to shield our kids from these stories. Yet these everyday experiences can become the basis for teaching values, and the way we adults handle them determines what values our children will adopt as their own. To fail to discuss someone's public drunkenness, for example, teaches that we place no value on sobriety. Laughing at such a calamity teaches that we enjoy others' misfortune. The involvement of the parents and the way they discuss these incidents is the key. These are the discussions upon which character is built; they create impressions that kids will take with them into the future and throughout their lives. There is no better way—perhaps no other way—to teach values.

I still remember a high school basketball game I attended as a freshman with one of my friends and his parents. During the game there was some booing of the referees from the student section. On the way home, my friend's father, Mr. Bondhus, assumed we had participated and told us in no uncertain terms that referees, like other officials, should be respected. Such behavior was wrong and was not to be repeated. For the rest of our high school days if refs were booed, Wayne and I were not a part of it. Mr. Bondhus had made his point.

In a similar vein, in the April 2001 edition of *Focus on the Family*, Dr. James Dobson said, "There is no sex education program, no curriculum, no school or institution in the world that can match the power and influence of … parental involvement. … [These] are the parents who are present and involved, who communicate and exemplify their own values and attitudes, who ask questions, who carefully supervise their kids' choice of escorts and points of destination, and who insist on a reasonable curfew."[3] Luke's father knew this, and Luke learned and profited from it.

Getting Teens to Talk

You may be asking how I was able to extract such sensitive material from teenagers. Men and boys like to sit side by side. So, I sit next to male patients, not across from them in a confrontational mode. It's kind of like the way men sit and talk at a bar or in a golf cart. Girls and women, on the other hand, are more comfortable sitting face to face or across a table or desk, so that's how I interview them.

I try to avoid complicated medical words and use phrases kids know and understand; sometimes, I even use the vernacular. When I talk about sensitive issues like drugs or sex, I ask first about what the kids at school are doing or what they think, then I'll ask about friends' activities, and finally I ask about them. Because they didn't hear me condemn their schoolmates or their friends, they feel comfortable talking with me. They know I want to hear what they have to say because I listen. Then they listen to what I have to say, and I say it without telling them they are stupid or wrong.

Sometimes it's hard to give advice without being judgmental; too often parents, counselors, and other adults withhold advice for fear of being perceived as judgmental. Kids really want to know what the adults they respect think, so I let them know what I think and they listen—but only after I have listened to them.

Parental Unity

Luke's dad also had the support of a loving wife who believed as he did. It is so important that we parents agree on the values we wish to pass on to our children. Certainly, no two people can agree about everything. Seeing one's parents disagree, have a rational debate or argument, and come to an agreement with which both can live is an important lesson. But when it comes to imparting values, parents must be united. Children without guidelines become adults without guidelines, and both can become confused and fearful, feel alone and unloved, and make poor choices.

It is especially important that divorced parents agree on the values they want their children to learn. Disagreement not only confuses kids, but teaches them that values are unimportant. Whatever conflicts you may have with your divorced spouse, take time to have a rational discussion with him or her and decide what values are important to teach your kids. Such discussions may be difficult, but watching your children face the consequences of their poor decisions is much worse.

Establishing Rules

Lynn Minton in her *Parade*[4] column reported on a youth from New Jersey who came from a house with no rules. This teen got into trouble with drugs at age 14. His dad said it was good to get that out of his system at a young age. Later, Dad was, "…understanding" when he began to have sex. At last the boy said, "… I turned myself around without any help from my 'understanding' father. You may think it would be great to have no rules and be able to do whatever you want. But trust me. I've been there, and *it's a lonely road when nobody really cares what you do*."

Too often we think of values as something ethereal or hypothetical; something imposed on us to curb our fun or lifestyle. But the values we're talking about are simply codes of conduct—rules, if you will—that have developed over time to protect us and society and to put order into our lives. These values include honesty; thrift; morality; respect for the rights, possessions, and lives of others; education; honoring parents; respecting the law; honoring our faith; respecting our leaders; etc. Parents who teach these values to young children make life easier for them. These kids know their parents love them and care about how they live their lives, and they tend to be looked on more favorably by society than the kids who don't receive this training.

Like people of all ages, teenagers need, want, and are searching for rules. Although these rules may vary from culture to culture, good parents provide boundaries and show their children how to follow them.

The most illustrative story I ever heard about kids listening to their parents comes from Father Richard Lopez,[5] a religion teacher at St. Pius High School in Atlanta, Georgia, and one of the best homilists I ever heard. He once asked his students to draw a picture of their conscience. "One drew a big circle," he recalled, "and in it the words 'my parents.'"

It is a parent's responsibility to help kids form strong consciences. Perhaps this is no more difficult than living the life you want your kids to live because, as Luke reminded us, kids listen to their parents and do what their parents do.

Mothers Are Important, Too

Many studies have shown, and we all have noticed, that boys who do not have exposure to fathers have a higher rate of incarceration. Likewise, girls who live without the presence of a dad have earlier initiation of sexual activity and a higher rate of teen pregnancy. Luke and his dad have shown us just how important a fathers' role is in parenting. They are a team who worked together with Luke's mom to make Luke the boy he was in that story and the man he is today. Now, let's talk about mothers!

There are many ways mothers influence the lives of their children, some subtle, some more obvious. On May 3, 1980, 13-year-old Cari Lightner was killed by a drunk driver. This driver had had three prior drunk driving convictions and was out on bail from a hit-and-run accident two days earlier. Turning Cari's tragic death into something positive, her mother, Candy Lightner, founded MADD (Mothers Against Drunk Drivers). MADD's mission is to stop drunk driving, support the victims of this violent crime, and prevent underage drinking. Due to efforts by MADD and other programs to reduce drunk driving, alcohol-related traffic fatalities have decreased from more than 30,000 in 1980 to about 17,602 in 2006.[6] This saving of more than 300,000 lives alone validates the claim that mothers do indeed save more lives than doctors.

In April 2006, an especially vicious tornado roared through Sumner County, Tennessee, destroying hundreds of homes, killing nine, and injuring scores of others. We were living in the area at the time, and the tornado missed our home by less than half a mile; but Amy and Jerrod Hawkins weren't so lucky. Their home was totally destroyed: ripped from its foundation and pulverized into a pile of rubble. Fireman Jerrod was at work watching the storm on local radar. As soon as the storm passed, emergency vehicles were sent into the area. When rescue workers arrived at what was left of the Hawkins' house, they found Amy lying on top of her sons in what was once the basement of their home. Using her body as a shield, she had covered Jair and Cole and prevented them from getting crushed by bricks, lumber, and other debris. But in the few seconds of the storm's wrath, she suffered punctured lungs, multiple rib fractures, a serious head injury, and permanent paralysis from a fractured vertebra. Mrs. Hawkins had sacrificed herself to protect her family. Her sacrifice didn't go unnoticed. In October of that year, she and her family were on national television. "Extreme Makeover: Home Edition" sent them to Disney World while Ty and thousands of Tennessee volunteers built them a new, wheelchair-accessible home.[7]

Another amazing show of courage occurred on September 4, 2007. Angela Silva of Fremont, California, threw herself between her infant son and a 60-pound pit bull. She received multiple bites which shredded the muscles of her arms and opened her forearm to the bone. Her screams alerted workmen at a house across the street. They were able to get the pit bull off of Angela and save her and the baby. Had she not been willing to sacrifice herself, her baby would surely have been killed.[8]

Not all mothers are called upon to risk their lives like Amy Hawkins and Angela Silva did, but they sacrifice in many other ways. Ask around; you'll frequently hear inspirational and heart-warming stories about the sacrifices mothers have made for their children.

Setting the Tone

On a less sobering and more subtle note, mothers set the tone of a home. Furthermore, there is scientific proof that a mother's mood can determine the mood of her children. According to a 2006 study in New York, children whose mothers were depressed had a two to three times greater risk of being depressed, anxious, or acting out violently than children whose mothers were not depressed. Treatment of the mother with antidepressant medication resulted in resolution of the children's symptoms within three months[9].

Another recent study showed that women who were stressed during pregnancy had a greater risk of having a baby with colic.[10] Believe me; a screaming infant who cannot be comforted is very stressful. I'm not sure if a constantly crying baby is the result of the mother's tension, but a colicky baby can prolong anyone's anxiety—dad and doctor included!

In the South we say, "If Mama ain't happy, ain't nobody happy." Lindsey O'Connor[11] has a book by that name, as do Kris and Brian Gillespie.[12] These books show how mothers can find joy and happiness in ordinary living and thereby provide a family with a positive attitude. The Gillespies list 52 rules Dad should follow to make sure his wife is happy. It strikes me that if Dad determines mother's happiness, then it's Dad who sets the tone; but that's not the message the Gillespies or the O'Connors deliver. They indicate that while Dad's role in setting the family's mood is important, the home will more likely reflects the attitude of the mother.

Psychologists tell us that women are usually more emotional than men;[13] that they use their emotions to make decisions while men seem insensitive, calculating, and driven by reason. Because a mother's emotions are more visible, it stands to reason that her children will pick up on her emotional state as well. We all know families with happy, outgoing mothers whose kids have the same attitude. Likewise, unhappy mothers frequently yield unhappy children. The next time you are at the airport or any other public place, watch the people. You will commonly see sad, frowning women with sad, frowning children by their side and smiling mothers with smiling kids.

Dr. Kyle Pruett is a prominent child psychiatrist at Yale Child Study Center and is considered one of the top experts on fatherhood. He and his child psychologist wife, Dr. Marsha Kline, have written *Partnership Parenting, How Men and Women Parent Differently and How it Helps Your Kids.*[14] Among other things, they suggest you and your spouse learn how you are different because it won't take long for your kids to figure you both out: "Mom gives better hugs, but Dad gives us more candy." They suggest, among other things, that you occasionally have "Opposite days" where Mom acts like Dad and Dad acts like Mom. The kids will love it, and it will help both parents be more aware of the difficult role the other plays. Just one of their conclusions states: "Knowing that their parents feel and act differently, but they will support each other on all the big issues, and expect certain behavior, helps your child feel prepared for the world out there. So instead of feigning disgust with those who acknowledge male and female stereotypes, we should celebrate these differences in the sexes and see how much fun life can be."

If a man is a single parent, he needs to be sure his kids have a woman to act as a surrogate mother, just like single moms need to find a surrogate dad for her kids. Grandparents often volunteer, but an aunt, uncle or other relative, a neighbor, or even a good sitter can fill this position. So too, can a step parent.

The Influence of Mothers

I consider mothers one of God's greatest creations. It may sound sacrilegious, but God could have done it differently. He could have made mothers more like dads, or in some way made them less influential in our lives—but he didn't.

In her commencement speech at Wellesley College in 1990, Barbara Bush said, "Your success as a family … our success as a society depends not on what happens in the White House, but on what happens inside your house."[15]

Commenting on Mrs. Bush's remarks, columnist Cal Thomas said, "Home, not Congress or the White House, is where ultimate power lies."[16] I would add that this power in the home lies with the mother. Mothers have the opportunity to shape their families and their communities. In a poem published in 1865, William Ross Wallace summed up the feelings of many of us when he praised motherhood by stating, "For the hand that rocks the cradle is the hand that rules the world." Few of us may remember Mr. Wallace, but this line from his poem has become a well-known adage.

Tool 2

Trust

Honesty is the first chapter of the book of wisdom.

—Thomas Jefferson

Fall Sundays in Wisconsin are always great because the weather is wonderful and the Packers play. Some years ago one of those beautiful Sunday football games was interrupted by a phone call from the police. What had I seen or heard the evening before they wondered. They were referring to the trees in the boulevard in front of my neighbor's house and in front of mine. They were small trees, with trunks less than two inches across, but neighbor Bill Reed and I had planted them earlier in the spring and we were proud that they were still alive. During the night someone had run over them and broke them off just above the ground. I had heard tires squeal, but nothing else and told them so. The officer told me that the neighbor across the street had also heard the screeching tires and another lady farther down the street described seeing a red, cloth-top jeep in the neighborhood about that time. There were no suspects.

The next Sunday I had just settled into my chair when the door bell rang. I wondered who or what waited on the other side of what once promised to be a relaxing afternoon.

"Matthew!" I said as I opened the door. Then I noticed the dour look on his face and quickly added, "It looks like things aren't going so great. How can I help? Come in."

"No," he replied, not looking at me. "I can't come in. The cops sent me here to pay for your trees."

Then he stood there while a big tear splashed onto the concrete step, just missing his right foot. Matthew crying! That was as unbelievable as his running over my trees.

"Matthew," I replied, "Are you saying you ran over Mr. Reed's and my trees?"

"No, I didn't run over them!" he said emphatically. "*You can trust me … I give you my word* … I didn't do it! But the cops think I did and they said if I paid for them, nothing would go on my record. But honest, I didn't …"

He couldn't get the rest of the sentence out; he was too upset. And so was I. Why would they do this to Matthew?

"Matthew, I believe you," I immediately assured him. "I know you well enough to know you wouldn't do a thing like that. If you had, you would admit it and not lie about it, so why do they blame you?"

"Well, somebody saw a Jeep like mine in this neighborhood that night, and when the cops stopped me, there were leaves under my front bumper. I explained to them that I picked up the leaves when I drove near the creek to get dad's cows and ran over some bushes. My dad even told them that, but they won't believe us.

Finally, Dad said, 'Just pay it and get it behind you!' So I guess that's what I'll have to do. It's not fair though."

"Sorry, Matthew, I can't accept any money from you. And I'll make sure Mr. Reed won't either. Let me call the police and tell them I believe you."

"Do you think they'll listen to you?" he asked.

"I'm sure I can convince Mr. Reed of your innocence, and together we can convince the police. Bill Reed is a lawyer, you know; it's good to have him on our side."

"What should I tell the police and my Dad?" Matthew asked.

"Don't worry about either of them. Give me your phone number and I'll call your Dad right after I call the police."

Matthew heaved a sigh of relief. "Thanks, Doctor. I feel better now, and I wasn't even sick," Matthew replied, trying to make a joke.

"Let me know how it goes," I called to him as he ran to his Jeep. "And call me if anybody gives you grief."

As Good As Their Word

I knew I could trust Matthew. He had given me his word. I had known him for years. I also knew his dad and his wrestling coach and mentor, Don Kreuser. If either of them gave you his word, you knew it was the truth. So I called the police and talked to the detective on the case.

"Doc," he advised, "Don't be a fool! You can't believe what that kid says."

"Sorry to disagree with you," I said. "I make my living believing what kids tell me. And I believe Matthew is telling the truth.

"Well," he snapped, "I make mine NOT believing what they tell me."

I realize that a lot of parents would agree with the detective. That's a consequence of this age of pessimism. We believe the worst because in a few recent events, like the Sandy Hook School shooting, we've seen the worst. But the Matthew I knew was worth trusting.

After talking to Bill Reed and Matthew's dad, we waited; but we didn't have to wait long. A week later I got another call from the detective.

"You were right," he began. "We picked up Tyler Bradson and he admitted to running over the trees. Seems Bill Reed was representing a fellow who Tyler allegedly beat up, and Tyler wanted to get back at Reed. Your trees just happened to be in the way. Luckily, he didn't do anything worse. He confessed as soon as we brought it up. He'll be calling you to make amends. Let me know if he gives you any trouble."

Trust First

Matthew's story illustrates the question that ultimately confronts every parent or adult who deals with teenagers: "How much should I trust them?" You can't avoid this conundrum—it will always find you. So be prepared to respond with a set of values that measure what trust means to you, as well as what you want it to mean to your child.

The Capital Times in Wisconsin recently reported on using the Global Positioning System (GPS) to follow teens. An October 12, 2007, article said, "Transmitters can be planted in teenagers' cars making it possible to track the car's movements on a computer screen map. The block-by-block progress of the car can be watched live (real time), or recorded on a computer chip and downloaded and viewed later."

Proponents of using the GPS contend that it allow parents to know where their teens are at all times, as well as keep an eye on their driving habits. They say it gives parents peace of mind and most importantly, ensures the safety of their children. It might, but at what price to the child's emotions and character development? Teens are constantly seeking trust from their parents and this surveillance would call that trust into question.

Kim Allen, a father of two teenage boys, was quoted in *The Tennessean* as saying, "If you are tracking your teens, you are saying to them, 'I do not trust you to make the right decisions.'" In the same article, 16-year-old Mia McIntyre said the GPS "...[W]ould be like my baby-sitter... would make me feel like I'm not an adult almost, and it would disappoint me."[17]

Let's pray that surveillance will not be the future of parenting because spying is based on distrust, and distrust can be as harmful to a child as it is to an adult. Imagine how we would feel if our bosses placed monitors over our work stations. Would that engender belief in ourselves and our ability to do the work required of us? Or would it make us edgy, angry, and less capable of creative thinking? The answer is obvious. We might even start looking for another job.

Keeping Tabs on Teens

Having said that, there is still a need for parents to know where their teens are at all times.

In a December 15, 2005, column in *The Tennessean,* Dwight Lewis was talking about saving kids' lives when he asked, "If you're the parent of a child between 10 and 18 years of age, do you know where he or she is at this exact moment? Knowing where your child is could help save his or her life. …" He goes on to quote Nashville Metro Police Lieutenant Danny Driskell:

"In this age where we all have cell phones, it won't hurt for a parent to call up his or her child and say, 'I'm just thinking about you. I wanted to see where you are and what you're doing and who you're with.' A parent needs to know the names of a child's five closest friends or who that child is out with. I have a 19-year-old, and I'm nosey. I want to know what my child is doing and who he is out with."[18]

If you don't know where your child is or who he or she is with at all times, Driskell says you need to "change your way of thinking even if your child thinks you're a nuisance." [19]And Lt. Driskell knows what he's talking about. He's the one who has to knock on the door and tell parents their child has been injured, arrested, shot, or killed.

I would expand Dwight Lewis's advice: you should know the whereabouts of all the children living in your home, regardless of their ages. Find out where they are going before they leave and establish well in advance of their leaving, a time for them to return. This knowing does not mediate the amount of trust we have in them. We're not dictating where they can go or who they are with, but as caring parents we have the responsibility to help them make good choices in friendships and entertainment. After we know they are capable of accepting that responsibility, we give it to them, and then give them the trust they have earned. Then, by merely keeping track of where they are in case they need us, or we need them, we have peace of mind and they know we love them enough to be concerned about their welfare. As President Reagan said, "Trust but verify."

Honesty Is for Parents Too

Parents and kids need to realize that trust is not given, it is earned. We begin to trust kids in small ways in early childhood. Then as they mature and prove themselves trustworthy, we trust them in larger ways. Thus, trust grows as kids make more and more good decisions and erodes if they make bad decisions. Trust builds their confidence (and ours) in their ability to make good choices. Distrust leads to diminished self-assurance, resentment of authority, cover-ups, lies, and general distrustful behavior. To answer the GPS advocates: if you cannot trust your teens, you should not let them get a driver's license. It's as simple as that!

But there's more to trust than kids making good decisions. Parents need to be willing and able to trust. Some people are never able to trust others because they have been hurt by someone they trusted; others know they are not trustworthy themselves and consequently figure no one can be trusted.

The ability to trust (or not trust) can even run in families and cultures, passed on from parent to offspring by emulation. Distrust is often based on ignorance, hatred, and fear. Prime examples are the prejudices between Arabs and Christians; blacks and whites; Jews and Palestinians; Serbs and Bosnians—I could go on and on. But the distrust had to start somewhere, and it usually starts with bigoted parents who want their kids to share these negative values. However, education and experience can slowly change these perceptions.

How can we trust our kids if we are not trustworthy ourselves? What is a parent teaching when he or she says:

"If the phone is for me, tell them I'm not home."

"If the boss calls, tell him I'm sick."

"Tell your teacher you had a stomach ache and couldn't get your homework done."

How can we expect children and teenagers to tell the truth when their parents are teaching them to lie?

One of my friends told me a story of his 13 year old son Seth. He and his friend went with his friend's parents to a local sporting event. When Seth came home, he was excited to tell them about the game they'd watched. At the end he added, "And we saved money because Mr. Montgomery said if we slumped down in the car when we drove in the gate and said we were 11, we could get in for free. So we did, and he didn't have to pay for us."

Giving himself time to think, he asked, "Seth, do you think that was the right thing to do?"

Seth hung his head and didn't look at his dad. "No, Dad, but, I didn't know what else to do."

"You're right, Seth," his dad replied. "It wasn't the right thing to do. But if I'd been in your shoes, I wouldn't have known what to do either. It wasn't fair of Derrick's dad to ask you to lie. It put you in a real bind. There was nothing you could have done at the time, but I tell you what. Next time something like that happens just say, 'Oh, that's okay, I brought some money,' and pay for your own ticket."

"So, you're not mad at me?" Seth asked, embarrassed.

"Seth," Dad replied, slapping him gently on the shoulder, "of course I'm not mad at you. You did the best you could in that situation. Let's just make sure you don't get in that situation again. Okay?"

He and his wife made sure there wasn't a next time with Mr. Montgomery. If Seth and Derrick wanted to go some place, they took them.

What a heart-warming story which illustrates that parents are the fundamental teachers of trust, any other teaching is always secondary.

Honesty is the foundation of character. I knew that Matthew was being honest when he told me he didn't run over my trees, because I knew him, his dad, and his mentor Don Krueser. But I never really knew what it meant deep down to Matthew for me to trust him. I know what it meant to me. It reaffirmed my belief that teens can be trusted. They are worth the risk of trusting, whether we are proven right every time or not.

Trust cannot be an act of blind faith, however. It is an exercise that comes from extensive experience: how often and how long we talk to our teenagers, how they answer our questions, and how they show respect—these are all telling signs. Sex, drugs, drinking, Internet usage, friends, and smoking are some of the many topics upon which trust often runs aground. Yet it is our behavior as parents which show kids the right path. The fact is, they will do as we do, not as we say.

Matthew taught me that honesty and trust are issues that remain first and foremost in the adult ballpark. Our kids will never get a hit in that park unless we first set an example of honesty. Then we'll know that great feeling when we hear the words, "Trust me, I give you my word," and see a good teen like Matthew hit a home run.

Tool 3

Dinner

Sharing food with another human being is an intimate act that should not be indulged in lightly.

—M. K. Fisher, 1949

Rick was a burly 17-year-old with dark hair and a heavy beard that framed his face. He had the intimidating appearance of a college linebacker. His looks and gruff attitude would have made any high school running back cut for the sidelines to avoid a collision. But Rick did not play football, or any sport. He was a bit of a loner, most comfortable when he was thinking and writing.

In these post-Sandy Hook School days, loners sometimes scare us. We often worry about kids when they keep to themselves and hold things in. We're afraid they might explode one day and consume themselves or our children, like the young man did at Virginia Tech in the spring of 2007 or the man who wreaked such tragedy on Sandy Hook Elementary. Most times our worry is unfounded, and I wasn't worried about Rick. His goal was to be a philosopher, a poet, or perhaps both. His father, however, was another story.

I had known Rick's family for a number of years. His dad was a machinist who worked long hours and tended to be controlling with his family. I don't mean "control" in the sense of every father's role in providing a sense of direction on rules and relationships; he micromanaged them. Today, many parents may act differently because of outside events like September 11, Virginia Tech, and Sandy Hook; in the same manner, our children will respond to changing pressures and perspectives that occur inside and outside the home.

Time to Be Together

Rick was healthy and like many teens, he didn't smoke, drink, or use drugs. As we proceeded with his health evaluation I asked him, "How often do you have dinner with your family?"

The answer to that question is usually indicative of how far today's families have shifted away from spending time together. Many family members are constantly on the go. Both parents may need to work to make the kind of living they desire, to fulfill their career goals, or in many cases, just to survive. Their children are on the go, too, with soccer, dance, gymnastics, and all their other activities. For the family, that means added pressure on schedules to transport, deliver, and pick up kids; find time to buy groceries and cook meals; and somehow get everyone to sit down together and eat. Many teenagers also have jobs that begin after school and don't end until late at night. Sometimes parents are already in bed when their kids get home. They become like ships passing in the night, and their lack of communication makes it easier for unfortunate and sometimes tragic events to occur.

With these thoughts in mind, Rick's answer about the frequency of dinner with his family was unexpected. He said, "Every night, if possible."

His enthusiastic response made me wonder if something more was going on, so I continued. "And how often is that possible?"

"Usually five or six nights a week."

"That's good," I assured him, backing away from my suspicions.

"Not good," he corrected. "Great!"

"Great? Why great?"

"Well, *I think you should have dinner with your dad every night* because he's not mad when he's eating. You see, when Dad comes home from work, he's mad until we eat. Then he gets happy and laughs and talks about every-thing. He even asks about my friends. We always have a good time at dinner. But as soon as it's done, he sits down in front of the TV and grumbles if we say anything. Even if he's not watching TV I can't talk to him without him yelling that I did something wrong or forgot to do something. Sometimes he's upset because my hair is too long or my room's a mess or I need to do more sports or my friends are rude. Anything will set him off. It's like he's a psycho. Some of my friends say their dads are the same way. Why do dads get so crabby all the time?"

"I don't know," I mused; this aloof young man had really been doing some remarkable thinking. "Maybe they have a lot on their minds, or maybe their dads were always mad, and they're following that example."

"Well, I'm not going to be like that when I get to be a dad … if I ever do," Rick replied.

"Good for you. You can be whatever kind of dad or person you decide to be. I'm just glad you're such a great guy now."

We talked more about the influence of fathers on the behavior (both good and bad) of their children as adults. Although children often pick up bad habits from their parents, the encouraging news is that they pick up good habits, too.

Benefits of the Family Meal

Too many parents, dads especially, only talk with their teenagers when they're reprimanding them for something they did wrong. Luckily, it's hard for people to be angry when they're eating. John O'Sullivan, in his book *The President, the Pope, and the Prime Minister*, quoted Pope John Paul II as having said, "Difficult problems can often be resolved over a meal."[20] Rick never read that book—it was published a decade or more after I saw him—but he was still quick to pick up on the importance of a family meal.

When questioning teens, I found that those who ate fewer than five family meals per week were twice as likely to use drugs or alcohol or have sex while still in high school as those who sat down more frequently to eat with their family. Other factors may have been involved, but a study of 527 kids in Cincinnati showed that those who ate five or more meals per week with their family were better adjusted and less depressed than peers who ate fewer than three family meals a week. Furthermore, the kids who ate family meals did better in school, were less inclined to use drugs, and had better social skills.[21]

Joseph A. Califano, Jr., chairman and president of Columbia University's Center on Addiction and Substance Abuse, studied the association between family meals and drug abuse and concluded in the September 2007 quarterly report that "… preventing America's drug problem is not going to be accomplished in court rooms, legislative hearing rooms, or classrooms, by judges, politicians, or teachers. It will happen in living rooms and dining rooms and across kitchen tables by the efforts of parents and families."[22]

Researchers aren't sure what accounts for the difference, but suggest that family meals may help kids learn to deal with the pressures of life and maintain a close relationship with family members. Sharing stories about the day's events and hearing how other family members deal with their stress may be the tools that help prevent adjustment problems.[23]

Fortunately for Rick, his father was able to make meal-time enjoyable by suspending his controlling nature while the family ate together.

Scientists have also noticed that the positive effect of eating together was diminished if the family watched television during dinner. They found that families who watched television while eating ate more junk food, fewer fruits and vegetables, and drank more caffeinated beverages.[24],[25]

Influencing Future Generations

I did not realize how much good a family dinner can do until last year when our daughter Maura, then in her early thirties, wrote a piece for our family reunion (which we call a symposium). At the symposium dinner, which in this instance was held at our home, each member has to present a short paper on a pre-announced topic. That year the subject was food. Here's what she had to say:

> "When we were kids, almost all of our meals were eaten together, as a family, at this table. I have come now to realize, as I sit with my own children around my family's table, that meals aren't really about food; they are about the people who come to break bread together. Through our everyday meals, we learn about each other and from each other. When we were growing up, at our meals we discussed not just the events of each person's day, but also the social and political issues relevant to the times. We learned how to think, how to feel, and how to love. Now I can see that family meals help to build community. Each member makes time for the meal, sacrificing other duties, other work that could be done, to make time for each other. We bless each other … and honor each other through this sacrifice. Most times we do

> so willingly since we feel responsible to each other as members of a family community. …
>
> Today, we come to this table to celebrate our symposium meal. We look at the beautiful feast set on the table before us; Mom and Dad have said, 'Eat and drink, we made this for you.' The food is here for us to enjoy, to strengthen us, and to let us know how much they love us. Yet, this family meal is about more than just our family, for it is within the family structure that children learn that love and justice are connected. The love shared between parents and the love they have for their children must flow outward from the family into social, civic, and political commitments. Families must first gather as communities of love in their own homes before they can be communities of love for the world. … It is our calling as a family."

Wow! Who knew my kids were taking so much from a meal their mother and I took for granted. My daughter knew, and so did Rick. A lot of good things can be passed on to our children through family dinners.

Tool 4

Pets

I had rather hear my dog bark at a crow than a man swear he loves me.

—Beatrice. "Much Ado about Nothing", Shakespeare, 1598

I became acutely aware of the worth of pets while I was at work one summer day. It was the most perfect day God ever created, and I longed to be outside where the air was clear and the birds were singing. The golf course, my garden, and the stadium all called to me. But I was stuck in the office, feeling sorry for myself, attending to dull, boring, routine cases that only yesterday had seemed interesting and exciting. How could I stay inside for the rest of this glorious day? I needed inspiration.

When I finally finished the long morning schedule, I carried my lunch to the office patio and munched my sandwich. A mocking bird serenaded from a nearby wire as I watched the cotton clouds make pictures in the sky. The other doctors and all the staff had stayed inside to escape the heat, so I was alone to enjoy the summer sunshine, contemplate what a good life I had, and feel bad that I had to go back inside.

"Hey, Dr. Donahue!" a voice interrupted my reverie. "Do you have a second?"

I looked up to see a pleasant young girl walking toward the patio. When I recognized her, I stood and answered. "Hi, Emily. Good to see you. Come and sit down."

Emily was a 16-year-old patient of mine. Her short hair was bleached from the sun and the pool, and she wore white tennis shorts that accented her tan. I thought I should tell her to be careful of the sun and use more sun screen, but I reminded myself that she didn't come for a lecture.

"I came over with Mom to pick up her prescription and hoped you would be here," she said cheerfully. "I want you to meet someone." She gestured to the dog she had on the end of a short leash. "Remember, I told you about him the last time I was in."

I pretended to remember. "Sure, but I forgot his name."

"Ogley."

"You're a right handsome fellow, aren't you Ogley?" I said, petting the top of his head. "How did he get that name?"

"Well, both my parents teach at Oglethorpe University and we got him from one of my mom's friends there. Ogley is his nickname. His real name is Oglethorpe."

"How long have you had him?"

"I got him for my birthday when I was ten." She sat down under the market umbrella and took off her sunglasses. She lifted Ogley to her lap and rubbed his neck. He kissed her on the lips. "I suppose you think that's unsanitary," she said without embarrassment. Then added, "It's better than kissing a dumb boy!" Her mood shifted abruptly and tears welled up in her eyes.

"Sounds like you broke up with your boyfriend," I suggested.

"Who told you?"

"Ogley."

"Well, I did, or I should say he did." Now the tears were really starting. Ogley went to work. He gazed at her as she talked, then he nudged her neck. He licked away her tears as they formed, all the while nuzzling her on the neck. Then, when he thought she had cried long enough, he nibbled on her ear lobe. With that she giggled and pulled herself together. Finally she looked at me and said, "I just can't stay sad or mad when Ogley's around. He always understands. *People should be more like dogs*."

"Want to tell me what happened, or should I ask Ogley?"

"I really just wanted to show you Ogley, but since you ask, I was just sitting in math, the last class of the day, and Jason passed me this note saying, 'Let's break up!' I just shrieked. All the kids looked at me, but I couldn't keep from crying. When the bell finally rang I ran to him, but he wouldn't even talk to me. I even cried on the bus. As soon as I got home, Mom was all over me with, 'Why are you crying?' and 'What's wrong?' and everything. So I told her we broke up and she was like 'Oh, I knew you would. Can you get your laundry done before dinner?' or something weird like that. I just kept crying and ran to my room. Luckily, Ogley followed me. I told him the whole story. He listened to every word and looked at me like, 'I'm the one who loves you.' Then he made me laugh, got his ball, and wanted to play.

"I know my mom loves me, but she just doesn't understand the way Ogley does. It always feels so good to play catch with him. Jason wouldn't ever play ball with me. 'Girls aren't good enough to play ball with boys.' He actually said that. Now I'm glad we broke up. But I wouldn't have been able to get through it without Ogley."

"Boys can be mean, can't they? Sure is good you have such an understanding pet."

"Having Ogley is like always having a best friend around. I can tell him everything and he listens and under-stands. He never interrupts, never gets mad at me, never tells me what to do, and is always there when I need him."

Emily knew what she was talking about. Dogs show compassion, loyalty, and unconditional love. Sometimes, having a dog or other pet can be even better than having a best friend.

Benefits of Owning a Pet

Studies have shown what pet owners have always known; having a pet helps us stay healthy. Doctors have discovered that adult pet owners live longer, recover faster after an illness or injury, and are happier than adults who do not have a pet.[26] Kids who have a close relationship with a pet have an easier time coping with the stresses of life.

The American Academy of Pediatrics (AAP) in a February 2009 statement about ways to love your kids said, "Owning a pet can make children with chronic illnesses and disabilities feel better by stimulating physical activity, enhancing their overall attitude, and offering constant companionship."[27]

A study in 2002 showed that infants who are exposed to dogs and cats have fewer allergies as children.[28] The finding was completely at odds with the "old doctor's tale" that families with a history of allergies should not have pets. Interestingly, further studies,[29] including one published in February 2008, have supported this finding.[30] The medical profession now knows that the presence of a dog or cat in the home decreases the risk of allergies and asthma.

Psychologists and psychiatrists have discovered that pets can help their patients get better faster. It seem that people seeing therapists are more comfortable talking about sensitive issues while holding, petting, or just being near a pet.[31] Many therapists have dogs in their offices and use these dogs to help their patients relax. The grandmother of our family dog Belle works with a psychotherapist in Hudson, Wisconsin. I haven't met Belle's grandmother, but if she's anything like Belle I'm sure she's an excellent therapist.

Margaret Pepe, the mental health officer for the American Red Cross relief operation after the September 11 World Trade Center disaster, worked with some 100 therapy dogs and 3 therapy cats. She was quoted as saying,

"I oversee 175 counselors: psychologists, and social workers, and I wish they all had four feet. The dogs are incredibly effective. I'm jealous of the four-footed therapists and their ability to engage and relax people in a matter of minutes."[32]

Pets help with physical illnesses as well. Dr. Karen Allen, a research scientist in Buffalo, New York, showed that having a pet helps decrease heart rate and blood pressure. She divided highly stressed stockbrokers into two groups; one group was treated with the usual high blood pressure medicine while the other group was given the same medicine plus a pet dog or cat. After six months, the pet group had a much lower response to stress than the group treated with medication alone. "Petting a dog has a dramatic and significant effect on a person's blood pressure,"[33] she said.

Pets, especially big dogs and horses, encourage their owners to exercise. Exercise, as we all know, has many health benefits; it reduces the incidence of obesity, decreases the risk of heart attack, and helps control blood pressure. Running advocate Jeff Fisher of The Mental Health Association of Middle Tennessee claims it helps control emotions. "[Running] helps me concentrate better at work, sleep better at night, and maintain a positive outlook on my life."[34]

My neighbor, marathon runner Jack Curran, used to take his golden retriever with him when he ran. She provided companionship for him as well as protection.

Some dogs can even help kids learn to read. My grandsons go to a school that has a yellow dog named Dusty. He is a border collie/golden retriever mix with black spots on his feet. He loves to sit and listen to the kids read. He is never critical of the reader and is interested in anyone who pays attention to him. Consequently, the kids love to read to him. By reading more the children improve their reading skills, which results in a boost to their self-confidence.

One group of psychiatrists in Knoxville, Tennessee, helped delinquent boys get dogs from the pound. The boys lived with, cared for, and soon learned to love their dogs. In turn, the dogs taught the boys structure, responsibility, and discipline.[35] Now many homes for delinquents have in-house pets to help the kids grow into responsible adults.

Dogs and cats are not the only pets people acquire: birds, fish, turtles, guinea pigs, hamsters, horses, and even snakes are kept by families as pets. When I was a seven-year-old we lived on a farm in Minnesota where, among other things, we raised sheep. One year, for reasons unknown to me, a baby lamb was abandoned by her mother and no other ewe (mother sheep) would accept her. At about the same time, another ewe had twins. But she died the next day.

Dad did what any caring shepherd would do and brought the three babies into our house. He placed them in a box in the kitchen and assigned us four older kids (ages five to ten) to care for them. After he purchased some black nipples from the farm store, we attached them to used syrup bottles and nursed the babies many times during the day and night. We grew to love these lambs, but Mom didn't! I suppose she wasn't happy sharing her tiny house with three four-footed creatures. Fortunately, a couple of weeks later the weather warmed and the lambs started sleeping through the night, so we moved them outside.

We also had a big mutt dog named Shep who slept on the porch in the warm weather, but he could turn the latch on the front door. Since there were no locks, he could come in whenever he wanted. One summer Sunday when we went to church, a thunderstorm came up and frightened Shep. He opened the door and invited his friends—Whitey, Blackie, and Bucky (names we had given the three sheep) — in out of the rain. When we got home from church, most of the family broke into fits of laughter at the sight of almost full-grown sheep in the living room. Mother, however, was not amused.

Our family has told this story hundreds of times and it never fails to send us into fits of laughter. Now, more than half a century later, Mom finally sees the humor in it. The point of the story is that pets of any kind provide material for conversation and laughter as well as instruction in responsibility and compassion.

My mother would not forgive me if I didn't say a word about pets as members of the family. She frequently got upset when she saw families who seemed to give more attention to their pets than they did to each other. "It's a shame that people spend so much on a dumb animal when there are so many starving kids in the world," she would say. And I agree with her, to a point. If a family is neglecting their children (whether they have a pet or not), they should be referred to the county's Department of Family Services and get the help they need. But the truth of the matter—even if Mom doesn't like it—is that people do have pets, pets do help families and kids in many ways, and 87 percent of families consider their pet to be a member of their family.[36]

If you own pets, you know that they frequently help you and your family laugh more, converse more, develop better attitudes, and have more fun.[37] Kids easily identify with them since animals are non-judgmental and see people for what they are, without any pretense—qualities families can emulate. "Companion animals may teach a child responsibility, encourage caring attitudes and behavior, provide companionship, security, comfort, amusement, or an outlet for affection."[38] And there's always the likelihood that as a child matures, because he or she cared for a pet that provided unconditional love, they will learn to love and care unconditionally as well.

Give a Little Love

One of our basic needs is to touch and be touched. Babies who are not touched do not develop normal emotions, and they often do not grow and thrive.[39] Nurseries that take care of sick and premature newborns have volunteers who come and hold them for just that reason.

Many families are "huggers and kissers," but other people do not feel comfortable being touched, not even by another family member. Yet they still have the emotional need of touch. Victims of sexual abuse especially are reluctant to be touched.[40] These otherwise healthy adults can satisfy this basic, biological need by having a pet. The touch of an animal is considered safe and non-threatening and can be an important part of their recovery. If pets are important in these cases, think how much they would benefit a normal, healthy family.

As much as pets give, they need attention, too. When we give our family a pet, we need to make sure we budget for veterinarian bills, food bills, and toys. American pet owners spent more than $53 billion in 2011 on the care of their pets. Even with that expense, 62 percent of American households own a pet.

If you have a family pet, make sure your kids help care for it and exercise it, just like they help with other chores around the house. Dr. Kris Bulcroft, a family researcher, found that mothers are more often the ones responsible for the children's pets, and dads are usually the ones who take pets out for exercise. If parents do all the work, the children will not learn responsibility.

Emily's words of wisdom sunk in as I watched Ogley patiently waiting for Emily to leave. "You know Emily," I commented, "dogs really are good for people. Our dog Belle is one of more than 400 trained therapy dogs in and around Atlanta. These dogs and their owners visit residents in nursing homes and hospitals. Belle has been chosen to visit the sick kids at Children's Hospital. I wish you could go with her to see how the kids, parents, and staff light up when Belle visits. She is such a sweet little dog, a lot like Ogley, but only about a fourth his size."

As we talked, Emily's mother came out of the clinic with her prescription. "Are you three about finished?" she asked.

"Hi, Mrs. Patracuollo," I said. "We've had a good talk. Emily is a remarkably wise girl. You must be very proud of her."

"I certainly am. Thanks for taking time with her."

I walked Emily and her mom to the car and then went back to my afternoon schedule, refreshed not only by the beautiful summer day, but by another very wise teenager. If you have a dog for a pet, you will understand why Emily thought we should try to be more like our canine friends. What a wonderful world it would be if we all wagged more and barked less.

Parenting Tips

- Be the person you want your child to become.
- Know where you stand, and let your kids know where you stand. Tell your kids enough about your life that they will know and understand how you obtained the values you have. Establish rules and teach them the consequences of breaking them.
- Accept responsibility for your behavior. Make no excuses, and accept no excuses for bad behavior.
- Respond to news items—national, local, neighborhood, school, friends, and family—as "teaching moments."
- Be truthful and trusting. If you are not trustworthy, you cannot trust others. Nor can you expect your kids to be trustworthy. There is no substitute for always telling the truth.
- Anticipate and model good behavior. Kids do not know how to act unless you tell them and show them.
- Love and respect your spouse. Show your kids what a good marriage looks like. Even if you are divorced, show respect for your children's other

parent and work with her or him to present a unified set of values to your children.

- Eat meals together as a family. Having your kids help with the cooking and cleaning up will make them more appreciative.
- If you have the time, space, and resources, get your family a pet. Require all family members to take part in the care of their pet.

Part II

Religion

A cure has been discovered that will turn teenagers into better students and safer drivers. It will make them less likely to be involved with crime, drugs, alcohol, and premarital sex. In addition, it causes them to have better manners, greater self-esteem, fewer mental and emotional problems, and to live happier lives. Interestingly, this miracle has been around for some time but is being used less and less by today's society. What is this miracle cure? Plain and simple: religion.

Tool 5

Organized Religion

Clothes are our weapons, our challenges, our visible insults.

—Angela Olive Carter

Claire's mother should have been upset. I know I was when her teen walked into my office the first time for her annual exam. This was the 90s, and Claire was into grunge: the dress-like-a-homeless-person fashion (or anti-fashion) that emerged from the Seattle-Nirvana-Kurt Cobain music scene. Claire's interpretation, however, just made her look sloppy and screamed, "I don't care what you think of me!"

She wore "nature shoes," the kind with straps and no heels; oversized, shapeless, olive green pants; and a large, loose T-shirt. She had on white lipstick and heavy, dark mascara. Her hair had been dyed so often that it was straight, thin, and fragile. I think it wanted to be brown, but it was blonde with violet and pink streaks. Her fashion statement was even more depressing because Claire was really an attractive girl under all the grunge and makeup.

I was puzzled by the mother's apparent lack of concern. Had Claire been my daughter, I'd have been more than concerned; I'd have been alarmed! But this was the South, and Mom was a soft-spoken, well-dressed, polite Southern lady.

I thought, my work's cut out for me with this family. I couldn't tell what Claire was trying to be or what message she was sending her mother, but I was glad she wasn't my daughter.

I was so wrong about Claire!

The Church-Health Connection

In my specialty, I've learned that sometimes you know what a teenager is going to say and other times they surprise you. Claire surprised me—and taught me some very important lessons.

The exam went smoothly and without incident. Claire was bright and alert; she even laughed at my jokes and made some clever one-liners of her own. By the time we got to the health habits review I was starting to like her, despite her fashion taste—or lack of it. However, I couldn't help but wonder what I would say if one of my sons wanted to date her. On the surface, she didn't look like she could be trusted, at least not enough to date my son. I started my review questions.

"How often do you have dinner with your family?" I asked.

"Every night," she replied.

"Do you have any guns in your house?"

"Oh, no!"

"What is your grade point average?"

"I'm not sure, probably 3.7, maybe 3.8."

I didn't know if she was being truthful or just telling me what I wanted to hear. It seemed like she was telling the truth, but she spoke a different language than her clothing did. I wagered with myself mentally that I'd get her on the next question.

"How often do you go to church or temple?" I asked casually.

God and spirituality have always been important in my life, but that's not why I asked this question. If a teen has a firm set of religious principles, I know I can worry less about them having problems coping with adolescence. Knowing if a teen believes in God is also very important in dealing with any crisis that may arise. Parents whose kids are religious are at an advantage all during the teenage years.

I didn't expect Claire's answer. "Every Sunday and almost every Wednesday," she said.

Really? Was I not seeing something about this girl? Trying not to show my surprise, I continued. "How important is religion in your life?"

"Oh, very important!" Claire exclaimed. Then she added her own wisdom. "*Going to church helps you stay healthy.*"

That did it. I was wrong about Claire, or about what her fashion, lipstick, and hair were saying about her, anyway. I would like her for a daughter, and she could date my son.

Still, I continued to wonder why she dressed the way she did when on the inside, everything was so orderly. That question would have to wait. Claire's answer deserved an immediate and emphatic "Amen!"

Because sure enough, going to church does help keep you healthy. And it's not just religious propaganda; scientific study proves it.

Addictive Behaviors

A study of adolescents in Dade County, Florida, found that the only significant difference between cocaine users and their non-using peers was that religion was an important part of the non-users lives.[41]

Another study in North Carolina showed that college women with strong religious beliefs consumed less alcohol and were less likely to engage in risky sexual behavior than were female participants with weaker religious convictions.[42] It's not that the non-drinking participants were convinced they'd go to hell for partaking, or that a bolt of lightning would strike the Coors cans right out of their hands. Something to believe in, beyond your own pleasure and the moment, provides direction in life, more so than just following the crowd—which is actually moving in no direction at all.

A study from the University of Michigan concluded:

> "Relative to their peers, religious youth are less likely to engage in behaviors that compromise their health (that is, carrying weapons, getting into fights, drinking and driving) and are more likely to believe in ways that enhance their health (that is, proper nutrition, exercise, and rest)."[43]

At a National Institute for Health Care Research conference held in May of 1997 in Milwaukee, Wisconsin, Dr. David Larson offered many examples of how people with strong spiritual beliefs benefited compared to those without religious convictions:

- Hip implant patients walked sooner and farther.
- Elderly heart patients were fourteen times less likely to die after surgery.
- Illness and death from heart attack, emphysema, cirrhosis, and suicide were decreased.
- Youths had a lower use of alcohol and drugs.
- Released prisoners were less likely to return to a life of crime.

Medical schools have recognized the importance of religion and its effects on health. Students now look at spiritual issues throughout the four years of medical school, learning practical ways to integrate spirituality into their practices.

Yet despite the evidence connecting religion and health, not all educational institutions are open to religion. In a 2002 article in *The New York Times*, Eric Goldscheider quoted David K. Scott, a former research physicist and ex-chancellor of the University of Massachusetts in Amherst, as having said he feared "that constitutional prohibitions against promoting religion had been used to effectively banish religion from public universities, or at least to 'ghettoize' religion in departments where it can be safely ignored by those who do not study it." Goldscheider went on to say that Scott "would like to see universities revamp the general education requirement to include courses and activities that challenge students to think about 'how to live, how to be with each other, how to be in the universe.'" [44]

It's no longer fashionable to speak of spirituality and religion in our society where the news media and politicians promote a secular faith instead of a personal one. But it's how people, particularly young people, personally apply religious beliefs that make a positive difference in their health.

Making Connections

Too many of today's children seem unable to forget themselves long enough to develop the empathy, compassion, and love of others that is needed to maintain a sensible, caring society. According to the Commission on Children at Risk, children and teens are experiencing a "lack of connectedness ... to other people."[45] The commission said they lack "deep connections to moral and spiritual meaning." This commission, supported by Dartmouth Medical School, the YMCA, and the Institute for American Values, claims that humans were created with a built-in need for close relationships with other people. We "are born with a built-in capacity and drive to search for purpose and reflect on life's ultimate ends."[46]

The need for attachment starts with parents and spreads to other family members; and as the child grows, it extends to the community. But instead of developing this closeness, infants are placed into infant seats, fed in infant seats, and carried in the same seats. I call these "slop-pail babies." I have seen mothers and fathers of four- to five-month-old infants who do not know how to hold a baby. To make matters worse, these same infants are placed in front of the television in their infant seats. This leads to what Child Psychiatrist Robert Shaw calls "… unattached, uncommunicative, learning-impaired, and uncontrollable children." Furthermore, Shaw says this denies children "the connections and rituals and nurturing that are so necessary to children's healthy development."[47] These connections are the basis of loving. Through them we learn to care, share, have compassion, and love.

Kids of every age seem to be disconnected. They sit beside each other and watch television or a movie; they text message rather than speak face to face; boys especially give a "high-five" rather than a hand shake, pat on the back, or hug; they line dance or do a twist type of dance, gyrating in front of others without touching or connecting with anyone, and many "dance" alone (perhaps that is why they feel the need to connect sexually—they substitute sexual intimacy for emotional intimacy). Many teenagers feel lonely and unloved. Consequently, they do not know how to love.

However, Robert Shaw went on to say that there are worse mistakes parents can make than failing to provide "connectiveness" for children. One of their biggest mistakes according to Shaw is "not conveying to your child—through both actions and words—the moral, ethical, and spiritual values you believe in (or not having moral, ethical, and spiritual values in the first place)." [48]And I agree. Kids who are not taught these values are left with a moral vacuum that is quickly filled with the amoral and sometimes immoral flotsam and refuse perpetrated on them by the media and secular society in general.

The only answer is to get yourself involved in a religious community long before your first baby is born, practice that religion, and when your first baby is born, introduce him to that religion at once. Live your religion and, as St. Benedict is quoted as saying, "Preach the gospel all the time, but use words only if absolutely necessary." Although that quote has also been attributed to St. Francis of Assisi, it doesn't matter who said it. It tells us once again that what you do is more important than what you say.

Your religious community should fit the definition established by the Commission on Children at Risk as "a social institution that is warm and nurturing; establishes clear limits and expectations; is multigenerational; has a long-term focus; reflects and transmits a shared understanding of what it means to be a good person; encourages spiritual and religious development; and is philosophically oriented to the equal dignity of all persons and to the principle of love of neighbor."[49]

If you don't belong to a religious community, talk to a respected neighbor, friend, or relative and ask them to sponsor you into their church, and get studying so you can help your children grow and thrive.

When getting little children involved in religion, remember that kids like to have fun. Use arts and crafts to illustrate a point. Teach them how to pray, morning and evening and over meals, and demonstrate through your own prayers how they can pray for others and for things that may be troubling them or their family.

One form of prayer is a blessing, a lesson that a handsome Jewish boy taught me.

Blessings

For a number of years, Aaron was just "the little brother." I didn't know his family well, although I had taken care of his big brother, Adam. I was not seeing younger children at the time. Adam was a scholar but not much of an athlete; he was nothing special to look at and very quiet. But he was a pleasant high schooler and I happened to like him a lot, so I was looking forward to meeting Aaron.

When Aaron turned 13 and made his Bar Mitzvah, he came to me for his health exam.

"So glad to finally get to meet you," I greeted as I offered my hand. "I've heard so much about you from Adam."

Aaron stood, grasped my hand firmly, looked me square in the eye and replied, "The pleasure is mine, Sir."

During the habit review he told me about his devotion to his religion and I praised his involvement.

"Aaron," I said when we were through with the visit, "Your folks must be proud of you, and I'm sure your Rabbi is, too. I wish I were your Rabbi so I could bless you."

"Thanks," he said, as his face blushed at the compliment. "But, you don't have to be a Rabbi to give me a blessing. *Anybody can bless anybody, any time.*"

"You're absolutely right. Could I bless you before you leave?"

"Okay," he said. "I'd like that."

"May the God of …," I began as I started to place my hands on his head.

"Don't touch my hair!" Aaron interrupted, letting me know he was a typical teenager. He didn't want his hair messed up.

I blushed. "I'm sorry," I said, letting my hand come to rest a few inches above his head. "Let me continue. May the God of Abraham, the God of Moses, the God of all our forefathers bless you today and every day of your life," I prayed.

"Amen," Aaron answered. Then with a wink of his eye he added, "Thank you. You might make a good Rabbi after all."

To some people my blessing Aaron may seem unusual, but when someone sneezes, most of us offer even a stranger a blessing with "God Bless You." In Tennessee, many people offer a blessing as a greeting. "God bless you," they say, and a friend echoes "and you, too." We're accustomed to blessing our food, our guests, our family, our work, and even ourselves; but other than at mealtime, how often do we think to bless others?

Even though I have often told parents that I would pray for them or their child (and more than once have prayed with them), I never thought to actually offer them a blessing until I met Aaron. I'll admit, many of us would feel strange holding our hands over another's head and blessing them. But a blessing does not need to contain a physical sign; merely saying "God bless you" is blessing enough for most people. It tells the receiver that you really do care about them and are thinking about them.

In the late 1970s I attended a sick newborn in the hospital. He was not the usual red color of most newborns, which is what tipped me off that things were not right with him. Instead, his skin was pale and his lips and fingers were gray. Cyanosis we call it. When I listened to his heart he had a murmur, and I was left to tell his still jubilant parents of the new baby's problems. After explaining the condition to them and answering their questions, they asked if I would call and ask their minister to come and bless the baby. I did, and in a matter of minutes Pastor Castels was at my side in the nursery. He, Dad, Mom, and I prayed for the baby and then for the family. The baby went on to have heart surgery and survives to this day.

It seemed strange to me that the parents and pastor thought it was special that I prayed with them, especially since we were of different faiths. I feel it only natural to pray (silently or aloud) with anyone who wants to join me. Why not ask God's blessing on His children? After all, isn't that what religion is about?

Establishing the Habit of Religion

In addition to praying with children, parents need to teach dependence and reliance on God. Every kid loves to decorate for Christmas or Hanukkah or other religious holidays. Even if kids are a bit messy, the fun of "letting them help", more than makes up for any "irregular" decorations. When they get older, let them light the Hanukkah candles or the Advent wreath. Make religion a part of their lives. Tell stories about your family going to church when you were a child. Kids of all ages love to hear family tales.

As children get older, be sure to take them with you to religious services and teach them the behavior proper for church. They need to learn to sit quietly, listen, and pay attention. That is not always as easy as it sounds. Many years ago my seven-year-old son misbehaved quite badly during Sunday Morning service. Although he didn't disrupt the service, he made it difficult for me and others near us to concentrate with his whispering, laughing, and moving around. After the service was over, I asked my wife to take the other children home as Brian and I would walk home after the next service. Brian was well behaved the second time and every time since. It worked so well for Brian that one Sunday evening years later, while we were talking on the phone, he told me that he and his kids had just returned from evening service. "We went this morning," he explained, "but the kids misbehaved, so I took them back tonight." He assured me they were much better. Not that going to church is a punishment, but it demands respectful behavior!

Amanda L. Aikman in the September 1995 issue of *Reach*, a magazine for Unitarian Universalists, relates recollections from her traditional Christian childhood:

> "I loved sitting in the eighteenth-century stone church with the adults and feeling very serious and grown-up. … I don't suppose I understood a tenth of what was going on in those services but they must have had some impact on me, because I remembered to pray when I had the worst crisis of my life. I remember falling to my knees on the tiles and thanking Jesus for letting me live."[50]

Kids generally learn and remember more than we think. Claire and I continued to talk about her health habits, goals, and ambitions. The more I got to know her, the more I liked her. She was a model teen with a delightful sense of humor—but a mysterious dress code. Although I wanted to quite badly, I did not ask her about her clothes; I had to remind myself that I was a doctor, not a fashion consultant.

Her mother returned to the room and I congratulated her for having done such a great job with Claire.

"We're so proud of her," Mom beamed, looking at Claire with delight and satisfaction. Then she added, "Did she tell you why she's dressed like this today?"

Claire's face flushed as she flashed an ear-to-ear smile, showing off her glistening teeth. I thought to myself, Please tell me, I'd like to know; I need to know! Please.

"Do you want to tell him?" mother asked daughter.

"No," Claire giggled.

As they left the room, Mom laughed and bid farewell with, "Teenagers, don't you just love them?"

I sure do. They make the world a wonderful, surprising, and yet mysterious place to live, where the faulty fashion of the moment on the outside can't touch the healthy faith of a lifetime on the inside.

The more I think about Claire the more I think she really taught me two lessons that day: the importance of religion in one's life; and (much to my embarrassment) not to prejudge on the basis of appearance. So thanks, Claire. I promise I'll be more thoughtful and less judgmental in the future.

(And Claire, if you're reading this , would you please write or call and tell me why you were dressed like that that day? I would really like to know).

Tool 6

Youth Ministers

I don't think anybody can be a truly successful parent without a commitment to an established religion.

—Corrie Lynne Player

Some parents think there is a disease—or at least a syndrome—that many kids get around 17 years of age called senioritis. They say it must be some kind of infection of the frontal lobe of the brain, the part that controls attitude. It strikes these soon-to-be adults quite suddenly as they enter their senior year of high school. Fiendishly, the infection destroys all the brain's worry neurons and boosts chemical levels of mellowing and confidence, building serotonin to abnormally high levels. Serotonin is the Alfred E. Neumann of brain chemicals. Alfred is, of course, the kid on the cover of *Mad* magazine whose motto is "What, me worry?" As an agent of senioritis, this chemical encourages teens to disconnect, have some fun, and take advantage of their youth, because after this year their future consists of becoming boring adults and either getting full-time jobs or going to college.

Somehow, though, Nicole and Maria avoided contracting senioritis. In fact, they elevated their attitude to a higher level and knew some lessons that many adults have difficulty grasping. I learned all this over lunch one beautiful summer day.

Influence of Religion

Nicole and Maria were daughters of friends of mine, not patients. I had enjoyed watching them grow up and since they were now between their junior and senior years in high school ("rising seniors" we call them in the South), I looked forward to treating them like adults. They were working as volunteer candy stripers at Children's Hospital that summer and at the time, my office was only a short distance from Children's; so I promised to buy them lunch one day if they could get to my office.

As it would turn out, the girls were much more mature than I had expected. Don't misread me here. I'm not using the word "mature" the way the media often does. That connotation is usually associated with teens doing reckless things with their bodies and futures; things like alcohol, drugs, truancy, and all kinds of sexual activity; things that can leave them scarred, dead, or taking a guest spot on "The Jerry Springer Show." The maturity I'm talking about is the character-building grit that makes parents proud and more hopeful that the next generation can avoid the just-stated kind of "maturity" that is eating away at so much of society.

The day began with a beautiful sunrise, which pleased me since we planned to eat at the Lake Side Patio Cafe across a small pond from my office. But I was disappointed when a sudden summer shower came up just before noon. In spite of the weather, however, the young ladies showed up on time and announced themselves to my receptionist.

"Please tell Dr. Donahue that Ms. Marvin and Ms. Brice are here to take him to lunch," stressing the "Ms." in order to say that they were no ordinary high school girls. Then they laughed in unison and turned to sit down. They hadn't seen me enter the lobby so I startled them when I said, "I'm sorry it rained. Now we'll have to eat inside."

"Who cares?" laughed Nicole. "A little rain can't keep us from being hungry. If we race to the café, no one will get really wet," she teased.

I accepted the challenge. We darted across the footbridge, jumped a small puddle, and dashed into the cafe. "Damn!" Nicole gasped when we got inside. "I got my shoe filled with water!" she exclaimed as she shook the rain from her auburn hair.

Maria flashed horrified brown eyes at Nicole. "Watch your language," she chastised. "There are adults around."

Since observing teens was my profession, I knew Maria wasn't really shocked with Nicole's use of a four-letter word. I'm sure they knew, and probably used, more. Kids usually emulate the language they hear in their homes or at school. Still, I thought I'd ask about it.

"Is that a bad word, Maria?" I asked.

"Well, my folks don't like it, and my youth pastor is against saying words like that, and I don't think he uses them," Maria answered.

"Well," I replied, playing Devil's advocate, "aren't youth pastors and churches against almost everything?"

"Oh sure," Maria replied with resignation. "But, they say it's best for you."

"Listen," Nicole interrupted with authority in her voice. "*Most things churches say we shouldn't do aren't good for us anyhow.*"

Nicole's comment impressed me. "Like what?" I asked.

"Well, take four-letter words. If you use them a lot, some people, especially adults, will think you're crude and they'll look down on you. Some even think it means you're a slut, and that can get you in trouble. It's like our minister preaches: we're supposed to live in moderation. If you eat like a glutton you'll get fat, and you know how bad that is for your health. Then there's sex," she added without blushing.

"What about it?" I asked, intrigued by Nicole's confidence and conviction.

"Our parents and ministers say we should wait until marriage to have sex, and if we don't, you know what can happen: AIDS, STDs, cancer, and pregnancy." Then she looked me squarely in the eyes and added, "Did you know that if you have an abortion you have an increased risk of breast cancer?"

"Yes, I knew that," I answered, "but I'm surprised you did. It's not a well-known fact. It may not even be a fact. Scientists are still studying it."

I really was surprised that Nicole knew about the abortion-breast cancer connection. Scientists have been wondering about it since the early 1990s when a study concluded that women who had one abortion had a 50 percent increased chance of getting breast cancer.[51] Women who had multiple abortions and a family history of breast cancer were at even greater risk.[52] Of 33 worldwide studies, 27 showed this connection while five were inconclusive, and one study in Denmark showed no relationship.[53]

A Harvard study in 2007 was hailed as putting an end to the controversy. It showed no increase of breast cancer in women who had had abortions.[54] However, Dr. Joel Brind, a researcher at City University of New York's Baruch College, and others criticized the study for a number of reasons.[55] First, the investigators surveyed women who had had abortion as well as those who had had breast cancer. Women who had died of breast cancer were thus excluded. To confuse matters more, the survey referred to miscarriages as spontaneous abortions—the correct medical term, but not one with which many women are familiar. Brind also noted that the average age of women in the study was 42, whereas the average age of diagnosis of breast cancer is 61. Furthermore, the investigators only followed the women for 10 years and did not include the 399 cases of carcinoma in situ, the earliest form of cancer.[56] That's like following a high school kid who smokes for ten years and then saying that smoking does not cause cancer. The abortion-breast cancer controversy is far from settled; cause-and-effect relationships are not always easy to establish.

Well-documented studies do show that depression follows many abortions. David Reardon, the American director of the Elliot Institute and a pro-life activist, in association with Jesse R. Cougle and Priscilla K. Coleman, compared data for women from the National Longitudinal Survey of Youth and concluded that women who have aborted a first pregnancy are 65 percent more likely to experience depression than those who carry a pregnancy to term.[57] This study and others like it have also stirred controversy. But even if abortion is found not to contribute to breast cancer or depression and in no way affects a woman, it has a fatal effect on the pre-born, developing baby whose life it takes. In this case it is well to remember what Nicole said, "Most things churches say we shouldn't do aren't good for us anyhow." The operative word here is "us"; she didn't say "me" or "you," but "us." And "us" includes all of God's children, both born and pre-born.

Know Your Religion

It is no surprise to anyone that kids begin to question authority during the mid-teen years. That's why it is so important for teens to understand as well as know the tenets of their religion. To help them understand, make it a practice to question your teens about why your church teaches what it does. Questioning helps them to think and, like Maria and Nicole, they will realize that religion is one of life's greatest allies. Opportunities to discuss religious beliefs (or lack of them) arise often from television programs, articles in the newspapers, and through ordinary conversation.

When parents take advantage of these opportunities, they pass their faith on to their children. But this is not possible if they or their children lack basic knowledge of their religion. Insist that your teens attend religious education programs whenever possible.

When I was practicing in Alpharetta, Georgia, I was impressed by the Mormon kids who began every school day with seminary (religious education) at five in the morning. These kids sacrificed early morning sleep to learn about their religion.

At the 2006 Memorial Day 10K run in Hendersonville, Tennessee, I saw a group of junior high and senior high school boys wearing T-shirts exclaiming, "I can do all things through Christ who strengthens me." The T-shirts were a project of their Sunday evening religious class conducted by their youth minister. These kids, like their Mormon brothers in Georgia, will have an easier time living a moral life because they understand their faith and have supportive friends. Youth ministry is very important in educating high schoolers in the tenets of their religion and in giving them a connection with kids who have similar beliefs.

The Role of Youth Ministries

A very comprehensive National Study of Youth and Religion concluded that "religion really does matter" to teens.[58] In this study, investigator Christian Smith found that devout teens hold more traditional sexual and other values than their non-religious counterparts. They have fewer emotional health problems, greater academic success, and more community involvement; they show greater concern for others, trust adults more, and are more likely to avoid risky behavior. On most of the measured criteria, Mormon youths were the most engaged in practicing their faith, followed in order by evangelical Protestants, black Protestants, mainline Protestants, Catholics, and Jews. Catholic youths were described as fairly weak "on most measures of religious faith, belief, experience and practice." The problem is attributed largely to ineffective youth programs and "the relative religious laxity of their parents."[59]

Many churches I know end all formal religious instruction when kids get to high school and replace it with a special Sunday night Teen Service followed by pizza, basketball, and other social activities. Social activities are important as they are the reason many youth attend church, but they cannot be a substitute for formal study. Many denominations have developed very successful education programs combining fun with learning. Smith's study confirms that teenagers need more instruction. Unfortunately, many teens are not getting it.

Finally, the study confirmed once again the importance of parents in teaching values. Lax parents lead to lax teens! If you want your kids to go to church or temple, you must go. If you want your kids to be fervent in their faith, you must be fervent. If you want your kids to have high moral standards and avoid promiscuity, you must emulate these qualities. There is no substitute for good leadership!

If your church has an ineffective youth program you owe it to your kids and to the community to step in and get things going on the right track. I am neither a cleric nor a theologian, but as a parent and a physician who has seen many, many well-adjusted youth, and too many teens in trouble, there are some things I believe every youth group should provide:

- didactic religious instruction in the tenets of faith.
- advice, especially by example, on how to pray.
- upstanding adult and peer role models.
- supervised social interaction with peers and adults.
- volunteer work in the community.
- the opportunity for one-on-one discussions with a youth minister or other trained adult.
- a safe place for relaxation, recreation, and fun.

I am sure religious educators would enlarge this list. This may seem like a lot to accomplish in the time available, but your kids are worth this and more. Insist on nothing less. Your kids may not like it at the time, but as adults, they will thank you.

Finding Strength Within

Lunch with Nicole and Marie was an eye-opener on several fronts. It was strikingly evident that it helps tremendously to have a friend who shares your morals and personal convictions. Nicole had Maria and Maria had Nicole. This made it easier for the girls—especially

Nicole—to speak so clearly and strongly about their beliefs to an adult, even on things like using four-letter words and having sex. That camaraderie also made it easier for these young ladies to talk about these issues with others, particularly those who did not share their beliefs.

"Nicole," I commented as lunch came to an end, "you preach a powerful sermon. I never thought about religion like that before. Have you Maria?" (I specifically wanted to ask Maria that question because sometimes one friend relies on another's strength to get along. And when friends are parted by high school graduation and different futures, the dependent friend can be set adrift in more ways than one.)

"Oh, sure," Maria assured me. "We talk about that a lot. It started after we had a sex education class in school. There are a lot of other things too, like drinking alcohol. If you drink in moderation—as long as you're an adult—you're okay; but if you get drunk you can do a lot of things that aren't good for you. Think, too, about telling the truth or telling lies. Which one is better for you?"

Alcohol is not good for teenagers because it poisons developing brain cells. Adults might benefit from a daily drink since it has been shown that alcohol increases the "good" cholesterol and decreases the "bad" cholesterol. But, the American Heart Association cautions people: "NOT to start drinking … if they do not already drink alcohol. If you drink alcohol, do so in moderation. This means an average of one to two drinks per day for men and one drink per day for women. (A drink is one 12 oz.

beer, 4 oz. of wine, 1.5 oz. of 80-proof spirits, or 1 oz. of 100-proof spirits.) Drinking more alcohol increases such dangers as alcoholism, high blood pressure, obesity, stroke, breast cancer, suicide and accidents. Also, it's not possible to predict in which people alcoholism will become a problem. ... The risk of alcohol addiction is always possible with some personalities and can even run in families."[60]

Religion News Service recently reported on the National Study of Youth and Religion, which has been described as the most comprehensive research ever done on faith and adolescence. Four of five teens in this survey of 3,000 teens and their parents said that religion is important in their lives. And among parents who said religion was very important in their lives, two-thirds of their children said the same. Most importantly, the survey said that teens with strong religious conviction are more likely to:

- Do better in school.
- Feel better about themselves.
- Shun alcohol, drugs, and sex.
- Care about the poor.
- Make moral choices based on what is right rather than what would make them happy.[61]

All too soon we had to finish our discussion of Nicole's philosophy and return to work.

"Before we leave," I said, "I'd like to buy you both an ice cream cone—if you won't accuse me of gluttony."

They laughed and agreed. The rain had stopped while we were eating, so we could enjoy our cones in sunshine as we walked back to the office.

"Thanks for the lunch," they said together as we stepped through the doorway. "We had a good time."

"I had a good time too, ladies. Thank you for enjoying it with me; and thanks, too, for the lesson in practical morality. Tell your folks 'Hi' for me, and tell them what fine women they have for daughters."

Now I know what some of you may be thinking. Perhaps these girls were just telling an old family friend what he wanted to hear. But they had so many elements in their characters that produce good moral decisions and strongly directed futures that it was impossible for me to overlook them. And there is no more important element than faith. All too often we think religion is somehow against us, not on our side, that the rules are arbitrary and make life more difficult for us. Yet as Nicole and Maria discovered, the truth is this: Religious rules are our best guidelines for healthy living. Let me quote a paragraph from *The New Harvard Guide to Psychiatry* that was published in 1988, but is still true today:

> "Many who have worked closely with adolescents over the past decade have realized that the new sexual freedom has by no means led to greater pleasures, freedom, and openness; more meaningful relationship between the sexes; or exhilarating relief from stifling inhibitions. Clinical experience has shown that the new permissiveness has often led to empty relationships, feelings of self-contempt and

> worthlessness, an epidemic of venereal diseases, and a rapid increase in unwanted pregnancies."[62]

This paragraph is only related to sexual freedom, but it is a short step from relaxed sexual values to permissiveness in all areas of life. Or does the road go in the opposite direction—from general permissiveness to relaxed sexual values?

Religious rules are guides to curb our behavior and ensure our happiness. Yes, life seems harder at the end of the teenage years so, the need to temporarily disconnect is understandable. But it is far better, more exciting, and a lot easier to simply find a guide to follow and plow ahead. Life is infinitely more enjoyable without the consequences of reckless sex, overdrinking, and overindulgence. Most churches have always known and preached these lessons, but some teens (like Nicole and Maria) just latch onto that wisdom sooner than others their age.

Teens, like people of every age, are searching for meaning in life and may at times get involved in religious fanaticism, cults, superstitions, or other over-the-edge religious fads which abandon common sense, science, and medicine. It is estimated that every month as many as five children die due to the religious superstitions of their parents or guardians. Some diabetics die because their parents refuse them insulin, some die of infections—pneumonia, meningitis, sepsis—because they rely on prayer to the exclusion of medical care. Ron DuPont, one of my good friends in medical school, said it is twice as hard to be good as it is to be bad because good generally follows the middle of the road, and there is evil on both sides. Relying on prayer without using the modern medical miracles which God has provided for us can be as dangerous as ignoring deity and religion altogether.

So, how do you get your kids to want to go to church and to continue going when they are in college or become young adults? Look at it this way: If you moved from Green Bay, Wisconsin and continued to be a Packer fan, how would you transmit this loyalty to your kids?

First, be a fan and watch the games. Remember action is more important than talk. Then, get some packer paraphernalia like Caps, Jerseys, and maybe even a cheese-head or two. Talk about the players at dinner and involve your kids in the conversation. Hey, gets some tickets and make a road trip to Wisconsin. By the time they are teens they will be fans.

Isn't that what we need to do to get our kids to be church goers? Go to church, have some religious things around the house, read some religious books, and involve your kids in religious discussion at the dinner table. You'll soon have kids who, like their parents are involved in their church and will become leaders in Campus Ministry. Try it, they'll like it!

The presence of faith in children's lives helps them develop that all-important moral compass that will guide them to happiness and fulfillment, regardless of age or circumstances. Faith will make them stronger, less likely to get a serious case of senioritis, and make us, their parents, even prouder of them.

Parenting Tips

- Belong to an organized religion and attend services regularly.
- Insist that your kids attend with you and are attentive to the service.
- Observe your religion's tenets in your home. Read religious books and view religious programs on television.
- Make sure your teens attend youth group or other structured religious education programs.
- Make use of those teachable moments to express your thoughts and your religion's views.
- Respect others' religions.
- Bless your children, your family, and your friends. It shows them you believe what you preach. Blessing even those who dislike you is even more telling.

Part III

Peers

How important are peer pressure and peer permission in a teen's decision to use, or not use, alcohol, tobacco, drugs, or develop other unacceptable behaviors? Is peer pressure a reason or an excuse? Do we parents, teachers, coaches, and other adults use peer pressure as an excuse for poor behavior? How does peer pressure differ from peer permission? Can peer pressure be a tool for effective parenting? The following stories will help answer these and many other questions.

Tool 7

Peer Pressure and Peer Permission

The child is the father of the man.

—William Wordsworth, 1802

Rafe was a bright, 16 year old boy with a GPA of 4.00 to prove it. But more importantly, he was street smart. He played trombone in the marching band, and although he had a lot of fun, he never got in trouble. He knew which kids to avoid and where to draw the line between fun and danger. He was the kind of guy you'd like for a friend, yet he didn't seem to have a lot of friends, just a few close ones who did things the same way he did.

"Tell me, Rafe, how do you deal with peer pressure?" I asked.

"Peer pressure? What peer pressure?" he answered as if I had conjured the term and problems associated with it out of thin air.

"Well, Rafe," I continued, "I see many kids who smoke and drink and a lot who use drugs, so there must be some pressure for you to do the same. How do you handle it?"

"How do you deal with peer pressure, Dad?" he replied. I thought he was a bit bold, but I went on.

"I don't have any peer pressure."

"Sure you do," Rafe corrected. "I work at the Country Club and I see some doctors come in every Friday night and drink too much, then get in their cars and drive home. I never see you do that.

"*Peer pressure is just an excuse to do what you know you shouldn't.*" Rafe concluded.

Birds of a Feather

I apologize for using an example from one of my sons, but Rafe's revelation was just too good to leave out. It was one of those moments that parents dream about but don't really expect to happen. Real life rarely provides clear moral-building episodes like we used to watch on "Leave it to Beaver" or "The Brady Bunch." It occurred when we were simply having dinner together as a family.

Now a sense of urgency surged through me. I needed to tell Coach Larsen about this. Seven years earlier, when our oldest sons started high school, Coach Larsen and I decided that if we expected our kids not to drink, we shouldn't drink either. We both quit, and at that moment it seemed that the decision was paying off. Still, I wanted to draw my son out further to hear more of what he'd learned from my example and perhaps, just perhaps, what he could teach me, his father.

"Rafe, my case is a bit different," I explained in my condescending adult way. "I'm old enough to handle things like that."

"Are you saying that because I'm 16 I don't know right from wrong?" Rafe responded indignantly. "That I can't think for myself or that I can't stand up for my own values? You know I'm right. Just admit it, and pass me some more peas. I hate it when you treat me like a first-grader."

I surrendered the conversational tug-of-war because deep down I knew I had already won an important battle.

"You're right Rafe, and I'm sorry. I know you have a working moral compass, but tell me why all the books and 'experts' are always talking about peer pressure?"

The question was my way of giving my son a sense of victory, too, something all teens long for. And judging from the answers he had already given, he deserved it.

"Well, Dad, experts should start seeing normal kids and stop comparing us to the weirdoes. Otherwise, it's like this: If you want to smoke or do something dumb like that, are you going to hang out with people who don't smoke and have them listen to you cough and tell you how dumb you are? No, you're going to find an idiot like yourself who smokes and you'll hang around with him and talk about how cool you look. No one comes up to you and says, 'Smoke this cigarette or I'll break your arm.' They usually don't even say, 'Smoke this or I won't be your friend.' Most of the time people don't care about you, or what you do. They only care about themselves. You can always find friends who want to do what you want—right or wrong."

Rafe may be a little cynical for his age, but his monolog convinced me that he has human nature figured out. And he has successfully applied his almost formulaic truth to an age group most adults don't put forth the effort to understand. Yet even if I could rent out a lecture hall for Rafe to repeat his truths to benefit those capitulating adults, how many parents would really listen to a 16-year-old with a bit of a smart mouth on him?

But Rafe's is not the only wise young voice out there waiting to be heard.

Peer Pressure or Personal Choice?

In her column, "Fresh Voices," Lynn Minton quotes 17-year-old Trent Collins as saying, "I hate all that 'peer pressure' nonsense. The major reason why I—or any of the people I know—started to do drugs was because we wanted to. Nobody ever talked me into it when I didn't want to."[63]

However, not all studies agree with Trent or support Rafe's theory. A study in the Bronx of 2,500 eleven- and twelve-year-olds indicates that for the younger kids, peer pressure was a significant factor, especially in those kids who had "difficult temperament and poor self-control and deviance-prone attitudes."[64] On the other side, a study of 90,000 adolescents from 134 schools across the United States concluded:

"Youth both pick friends who do what they want to do, and are influenced by those friends' behaviors ... the influence of having friends who smoked was enhanced by risk factors in other domains. This suggests that the association may be at least partly due to the influence of friends."[65]

Let me relate a personal story I'm not particularly proud of. Just before starting my senior year in high school, my family transferred to a new school district. I had been a popular kid in the previous school and was class president there for three years running. Now, as a senior, I knew no one. At the close of that first lonely week, I went by myself to the football game. In this small town, with a population of fewer than 400, our school was only a few blocks from downtown.

The junior varsity played at 6 p.m. and was followed by the varsity game. Between the games, the custom was to walk downtown and have a bottle of pop at the drug store. After the J.V. game, I followed the crowd to the drug store, sat by myself at the soda fountain, and drank my pop. Feeling a bit sorry for myself, I did not walk back with the herd, but lagged behind. On the way back I noticed a small group of boys in the alley smoking cigarettes. One called, "Hey kid, come over here."

A sudden rush of adrenalin coursed through my veins. I was not invisible after all! I didn't run to them, but I hurried. As I approached, one of the boys said, "We'll give you a cigarette if you don't tell anyone that we were smoking." Smoking in those days would get you kicked out of school.

"I won't say a thing," I answered, lighting up the cigarette they gave me. We made a bit of light conversation as they filled me in on which girls were available in this school and which ones I needed to leave alone. Then I walked with them to the varsity game, happy that I had found some friends. But satisfied that their smoking would remain secret and that I would not compete for their girlfriends, they quickly dispersed and left me as alone again.

I wish I could say that was the first—or the last—cigarette I ever smoked, but unfortunately, it wasn't. Many months before (while still in my old school) I wanted to smoke. I tried my first cigarette, and that first cigarette came from a friend's pack just like two-thirds of all smokers' first cigarettes do. Eventually I became a daily smoker, like nearly half of the almost 4,400 middle and high school students who start smoking cigarettes each day.[66]

A year later, I began the first of many attempts to quit; I finally managed it some ten years later when my five-year-old son said he wished I would quit so I wouldn't get cancer. I took his advice, threw my pack into the waste basket, and have not smoked since.

Now, some could say I started to smoke because of peer pressure, but I would agree with Rafe and Trent. If I hadn't wanted to smoke, I could just as easily have told the boys that I wouldn't tell, talked with them briefly, and gone back to the school. I started to smoke not because I was lonely, not because of the boys behind the drug store, not even because of my friends at my other school; I started smoking because I wanted to. Almost two decades before he was even born, I proved that Rafe was right.

My excuse is that we did not know then how bad smoking was for your health. It wasn't until 1964 that the United States Surgeon General Luther Terry released the Public Health Bulletin landmark report "Smoking and Health" describing the relationship between smoking and cancer.[67] The success of that report was unparalleled in public health history. Since then, adult smoking rates have dropped in half and millions of lives have been saved. Unfortunately, many still smoke; 25 million Americans alive today will die from smoking cigarettes.

Living without Peer Pressure

The kinds of truths Rafe and Trent recounted didn't constitute brain surgery. The simple truth is that if your teen's friends are smoking or doing drugs or having sex, chances are good that your child is, too.

Rafe's approach may be simple and a bit tough when it comes to human nature, but perception is reality; and if he and those who think like him don't accept peer pressure, then for them there is no peer pressure.

Years later I had the pleasure of having dinner with Rafe and his family. While my 15-year-old grandson Harry and I were alone on the patio, I asked him the same question I'd asked his Dad some 27 years earlier. "Tell me Harry, how do you deal with peer pressure?"

"Peer pressure?" he asked. Then he thought for a minute and replied, "I just ignore it."

"Ignore it?" I prodded. "I thought peer pressure was a big part of high school. Isn't that what the experts on teen behavior say?"

Not feeling any pressure to agree, he answered, "Grand-par (that's what the grandkids call me), I suppose there are some kids who do things so other kids will like them, but that's dumb. I just do what I need to do!"

Harry, like his dad, didn't even acknowledge peer pressure.

Peer Pressure / Peer Permission

There are probably three kinds of peer pressure. The most common kind is a desire to do something that is neither right nor wrong just to fit in or because others do it. In Tennessee wearing orange is an example. Vandy fans might think that's wrong, because orange is UTs color but, it really doesn't matter. Other examples are kids who want to wear their hair long or short depending on what everyone else is doing. Choosing a favorite soda, drinking coffee, wearing rings are some other examples. These things are value neutral and should not concern us. We may not like long hair on boys, but we let it go. It is not a cause worth fighting, so live with it!

The second kind of peer pressure involves wanting to do something that we know is wrong, but others do it and we would like to do it, too. Kids, like the rest of us, need permission to do the things they know they shouldn't. They seek permission from other kids who are already involved it that activity by hanging around them and perhaps even asking them to get them some drugs, cigarettes, alcohol, or whatever it is they want. We call that negative peer pressure, but we should start calling it like it is, "Peer Permission". I've talked with many teenagers who wanted to try marijuana. They sought permission from some friends who they knew smoked and tried it once or twice. But they did not like it so they no longer hang out with those kids.

Positive peer pressure, on the other hand, does exist! When we know we should do something but really don't want to do it, peers will "pressure" us into doing it in subtle ways, without even knowing it.

"Hey, Joe," they may ask. "Did you finish your report yet?" "Were you able to get problem 12?" "Wasn't that story we had to read interesting?" "Don't you just hate the way smokers stink?"

This pressure is real peer pressure! It's the kind of pressure which we should use to motivate our teens. Discussing a homework topic with your kids is more effective than helping them with the homework. If your kid is studying American history, you could engage him in some part of history you know. Perhaps your grand dad was in World War Two, or maybe you were in Kuwait. Tell them about it, ask them if they think it was a just war? Get them involved it. Then, let them do their homework; it gives them ownership and that's exactly what we want. Ownership is a great motivator!

The lesson in all this is to make sure kids know what is right, what is wrong, and what is value neutral; and why! By showing them your values and telling them **why** you believe in these values you will set the stage for them to not seek peer permission. They will not want to disappoint you, their esteemed parents! You will have conquered the dreaded "peer pressure" and realize it's peer permission that harms.

The old saying, "You're never too old to learn," should be accompanied by another adage: "You're never too young to teach." In our conversation years ago, Rafe became the teacher, and I marveled at him. As parents, we have to use Tool # 1 and take time to listen to our kids and their peers if we are to realize the wisdom they've acquired.

Don't be afraid to talk with your kids and their friends frequently about their goals, values, and habits. Keep communication between you open by not over-reacting to what they tell you. Then let them know your thoughts and values and expectations for them. Believe it or not, most of the time your kids do listen to you; and even if they don't show it at the time, they value your advice.

Sure, peers are important in your child's life, but your influence is so much greater. Use it! Connecting with your teens and their peers, not as a friend, but as a caring, loving parent is special to them. Make time for them; be watchful of their habits and the relationships they form. And never again accept "peer pressure" as an excuse for bad behavior.

Tool 8

Know Your Kids Friends

Faithful friends are a sturdy shelter: Whoever finds one has found a treasure. Faithful friends are beyond price; No amount can balance their worth. Faithful friends are life-saving medicine; and those who fear the Lord will find them.

—Sirach 6:14–17

The NBC-TV series "Friends" was more than a very successful Thursday night sitcom. A big part of the appeal was the model of friendship displayed on the series. It was how Americans wanted their friends to be in real life.

As much as anything else, friends reflect who we are. We pick friends who are most like us, who share our goals, or our lack of goals. Friends can be a sturdy shelter reinforcing our better traits—or our worst enemies who feed our destructive sides. For the years "Friends" ran on television, Rachel, Monica, Phoebe, Joey, Chandler, and Ross laughed together, cried together, and did fun and silly things together. They could act like themselves, say exactly what was on their minds, and still be friends. None of them did anything extraordinary, but they were always there for each other in every crisis.

Dogs and Fleas

Parents tell their teenagers that they'll be there for them no matter what happens, but a friend is there because he or she likes who we are and sees the value in having our well-being tied to theirs. That's an incredible endorsement of who we are as people; everyone, particularly teens, needs that kind of endorsement.

Sharing experiences with someone your age with similar character traits is critically important. We can't choose our parents, but we can choose our friends. Until I met Marc I thought choosing the right friends was no simple task; Marc told me otherwise.

Marc looked older than his 14 years. He was tall and thin with well-developed muscles and a splash of fine black hair on his upper lip. It was not enough hair to call a moustache but enough so that his mother, as mothers do, nagged him to shave.

He smiled (and she frowned) when I told him it looked cool. It really didn't. He knew it and I knew it. But if he shaved, who would know that he was fast approaching manhood and the kind of maturity defined by hair above the upper lip? Ah, manhood—that indefinable fantasy and urgency all teenage males desire and pursue.

"How did your mom ever talk you into a physical?" I asked, knowing that nobody, especially a teenage male, ever comes for an exam without prodding.

"Friday is my birthday, and Mom thinks I need to come in every year, even if I don't want to. And I don't want to," Marc assured me.

"Well," I confided, "nobody likes physicals. I don't mind them when I'm standing on this side of the table, but I'm just like you when I'm the patient. Your Mom is right, though. Men your age need to have a checkup every year. But you don't need to like it."

Then I explained the health evaluation process, a process that has allowed me to gain remarkable access into the teenage mind and the extraordinary thinking going on inside.

"I look at a checkup as having three parts," I explained. "First, we try to find out if you've been healthy, then if you are healthy, and finally if you're going to stay healthy. So, I'll ask you and Mom some questions about your health history, and then I'll examine you from the top of your head to the bottoms of your feet. Finally, to see if you'll stay healthy for the next hundred years, I will ask you questions about your health habits. Can you think of any habits that can help you stay healthy?"

"Sure, that's easy," Marc rapidly replied. "Exercise every day, eat right, and don't smoke."

No surprise there. It seems like all kids know these three, even if they haven't formed the habits. Marc's response was as routine as if he were reciting his multiplication tables.

"Sounds good to me," I told Marc and Mom. "How about some habits kids could form that would make them unhealthy?" I've asked this question often enough to know what his answer would be.

On cue, Marc replied, "Don't exercise, eat bad foods, and smoke."

"That's a good start," I assured him, following my good doctor script. "There are many others: fighting, drugs, alcohol, sex, maybe even arguing with your mother!" I added that quip to make up for the frown I induced from Mom in complimenting her son's mousy-looking moustache. She rewarded me with a smile.

"Let's get on with the first set of questions, then we'll ask Mom to have a seat in the waiting room while we finish the last two parts," I continued. "Remember, the things we talk about are confidential as far I'm concerned. You can talk to anybody you like, but my lips are sealed. The only time I would break that confidence would be if you had a rapidly progressing fatal disease or if I thought you were in danger of shooting a friend, or me, or somebody really important, like yourself. Are you both comfortable with that?"

Mom and son agreed and we proceeded. By the time we got to the third part of the evaluation, Marc was relaxed and talking easily. Now he felt free to break from the script and textbook responses.

"Do any of your friends smoke?" I asked.

"Not if they want to be my friends," Marc answered.

"How much alcohol does your best friend drink?"

"None."

"Do you have any friends who use marijuana or other drugs?"

"No. I have really good friends," he said proudly. "You'd like them." He paused for a moment and then asked, "Can I tell you something?" He leaned over conspiratorially, as though he was about to tell me where Osama Bin Laden was hiding. "*If you sleep with dogs, you'll get fleas,*" he said proudly.

"Hmmm, I guess you're right," I replied, but I really wasn't sure where Marc was coming from with that statement, or where he was going with it. I'm not a vet, I'm a pediatrician. So I repeated, "If you sleep with dogs, you'll get fleas means ...?"

"Well, say you're at a party and everybody is smoking pot, but you're not, and the cops come in," Marc began. "They will take you all away and it won't matter what you say. They and everybody will think you smoked too. So you will have their fleas, and no one will believe you're innocent."

Then he smiled that all-knowing smile kids use with adults to say "Gotcha!"

"That's great!" I exclaimed, trying to reclaim face for not understanding initially. I was in awe, too. "I wish I had been as wise as you when I was 14. Too bad all kids don't know that."

"Oh, they do," Marc corrected me. "They just don't want to admit it."

We talked a while about friends and peer pressure and all too soon the interview with this wise teenager came to an end.

The Wrong Kind of Friends

Later that day I saw one of my regular patients, Craig. He was a known troublemaker who had served time in the youth detention center for fighting, drug use, truancy, and who knows what else. I was seeing him for counseling.

I couldn't help but like Craig. With me he was charming and thoughtful. But I knew he could also be cunning, manipulative, and very anti-authoritarian. Perhaps he didn't see me as an authority figure, or maybe he saw me for the softie I am. In any event, we got along well. I saw him a number of times over the summer and by the time school started, he was willing to get back into the classroom. (I wish I could say he graduated with honors and went on to become the governor of Georgia, but he didn't. He did finally get his GED, and the last I heard from him, he was gainfully employed.)

During football season that fall, my sons and I met Craig in the runway leading to the football field.

"Hi, Doc," he said with a smile. "Good to see you get out of the office once in a while."

I returned the greeting and we went on. As soon as we were out of his sight, my 15-year-old son asked in almost parent-like disgust, "Dad, do you know who that boy is?"

"Yes," I said. "He's a friend of mine."

"Well, Dad," Sean replied in the same parental fashion, "You shouldn't have friends like that."

I was taken back a bit, but was able to come up with, "No, Sean, you shouldn't have friends like that."

Sean, like Marc, knew the value of having good friends and the danger of having the wrong kind of friend. I guess you might say Sean was worried that I might get "fleas" from Craig.

Yes, Marc had been right; teens do know about the dog and fleas analogy and about choosing the right friends. And they know ignoring that rule can have consequences.

On August 11, 2000, 16-year-old Kirby Cruce of Duluth, Georgia, was killed in a car accident while driving home from a party. Her blood alcohol test confirmed that she was legally drunk. The police raided the party some minutes later and arrested 41 teens for possession of alcohol. Later, in court, 21 of them pleaded guilty and were sentenced. The others entered pleas of not guilty and were given court dates to defend themselves. An article about the incident in *The Atlanta Journal-Constitution* stated: "All claim they were not drinking or even holding alcohol when police arrived. Police have said they charged everyone at the party, whether they were drinking or not."[68]

Just as Marc had told me three years earlier, no one believed these kids were innocent. Most people thought they were drinking, too; they got "fleas" from Kirby and the 21 others who were drinking. And poor Kirby lost her life—which is a tragedy no matter how you look at it.

I wish every teenager recognized the fact that they will be influenced by their friends. That's why picking friends who follow the rules is by far the wisest thing to do.

One last thought on the subject of friends. As important as they are, they need to know their place, and bedrooms are not it! Bedrooms are for changing clothes and sleeping, not for entertaining friends.

Imagine your kids' reaction if you had another couple over and you and your spouse disappeared with them into the bedroom and closed the door. That should be your reaction if your kids have friends in their rooms. Don't start a habit you will live to regret. I have known many teens that got into trouble in their own bedrooms while their parents were in the home. Your children's friends should remain in the family room, the recreation room, the living room, or any other public part of your home—never the bedroom. And finally, as unpopular as it may sound, I've found that "sleepovers" are a bad idea! Many high school kids have told me they watch porn, drink alcohol, have sex, and some even use illegal drugs in their or their friends' bedrooms during sleepovers.

Despite well thought-out strategies and careful planning, life-changing communication with children often comes when it is least expected. The only secret is to be there so that when it happens, you can positively reinforce what is being said.

I learned this one day while visiting a high school in Atlanta. The teacher had left the classroom, so I was alone with the students when a girl, a newcomer in the class, stole the show and changed a lot of lives in the process. She did this by answering a question that my mentors and colleagues had been unable to answer—an answer that was helpful to me, her classmates, and many kids I've met since. I'd like to introduce her to you, but I don't know her name or much about her since I only met her that once. For the purpose of this story, however, I'll call her Beth.

A Hard Lesson

I had been invited to talk to the sophomore class at one of the Atlanta area high schools. They were having a career day, and I was to represent physicians. I never pass up an opportunity to talk with students or to eat with them because that's when I learn from them. The invitation included lunch, so I left the office and set out for what was to become an educational day.

After a too-short lunch with a fun bunch of high schoolers, I proceeded to my assigned classroom and commenced my presentation. I only had an hour, so as soon as the short introductions were finished I started answering the many questions the students posed.

"How many years do you have to go to college to be a doctor?"

"Do you really have to get good grades in high school?"

"How long did it take you to get used to seeing blood?"

"How do you deal with people who die?"

"Aren't you afraid of catching something?"

"What do you do if patients cry when you tell them something is wrong?"

"Did you ever have a patient try to commit suicide?"

"Do you ever take care of people who have AIDS?'

"What do you do if patients don't follow your advice?"

And then the zinger from a girl in the back row:

"What should a person do if her friend is using drugs or alcohol?"

She obviously had someone in mind. This would have to be handled delicately; the offender could be in the room and my answer could affect a life, maybe many lives. Unfortunately, there was no one to help me.

"That's an outstanding question," I replied. "Let me ask the class what they think would be the best approach."

The room was dead silent. There was some shifting of feet in the back and a glance from a student on the right, but no hands up yet. Then a boy near the front on the left cleared his throat.

"I guess," he began, "if he was really a friend of yours, you should help him by, maybe, telling him that was stupid and he should quit." Then more confidently he added, "That's what I'd do."

"That's just plain dumb," a blonde behind him criticized. "How much good do you think you can do by telling him to quit? I think you should tell his mother."

"Narc!" someone from the other side of the room called out. It was starting to get interesting. Then he continued. "All you'll do if you tell his mom is get him in trouble and get him mad at you. Then his mom will call your mom and they'll have an argument. So, I say just let him be."

"Joe!" a feisty red-headed girl jumped in. "What kind of a friend are you? You're supposed to help your friends when they're in trouble, not abandon them. I'm glad I'm not your friend." She flushed in anger. "Besides, you're not getting him in trouble if you tell his mother. He already got himself in trouble."

"That's what I meant," the first boy interjected. "If you abandon him you can't help him. But if you're his friend, then you can help."

"How can you help?" a third girl chimed in. "We all know of kids who are in treatment centers and even with lots of counselors and doctors and stuff, some of them still can't be helped."

This discussion continued for quite a few minutes. Boy, this is good, I thought. But how am I going to resolve it?

Brothers and Sisters Keeper

Then, from the middle of the classroom, Beth raised her hand. I nodded to her and she stood up. Strange, I thought. She must have been in a private school somewhere before this. I never saw a public school kid stand to answer a question.

There was something special about Beth. Unlike most of the other girls, she didn't wear makeup. Her pale lips quivered slightly as she began to speak.

"Can I say something?" she asked softly. I nodded and she continued. "Most of you don't know me very well. I just moved here from Maryland two months ago."

She turned and addressed the class. "Let me tell you what I think, but first let me tell you why I moved here. You'll find out anyway.

"When I was living in Annapolis, both of my parents left for work before I went to school; so I just sat in the kitchen, bored, and waited for the bus. One Monday, after my folks had had a party the night before, I thought I'd try some vodka. It was still sitting on the kitchen counter, so I poured myself a glassful. I can't say I liked it, but I drank a pretty big glass of it, and by the time I got to school I was laughing, and everybody thought I was like a clown or something. I felt like, real popular, so after that I drank vodka every morning before school. It was easy because my folks always had a big liquor cabinet and they never seemed to miss what I drank. This continued for almost the whole year. It got to the point where I couldn't pay attention and would fall asleep in class. Before long, my grades were shot and I was in trouble. My folks didn't know what was going on until one day my friend said she had had enough of me destroying my life, so she called my mom. Then she told my homeroom teacher, and she even called the police."

By now Beth was in tears and the classroom was in a total hush. But she continued.

"The police were at my house when I got home from school. I was so scared I was shaking. If my folks hadn't been there, I would have had my usual after-school drink. Boy, did I need one. I was in serious trouble and I knew it. My folks put me in a rehab center and I was so mad. I swore I would never talk to my friend again; I would find some way of getting even with her!

"But, revenge had to wait while I went to rehab. When I got out, all my former friends thought it was really funny that I had been in rehab. They made fun of me and some even tried to get me to drink again. I mean everyone except the friend who had called my mom. She tried to stick with me and help me, but I was still mad at her and wouldn't even talk to her. The teachers didn't trust me, and I was eventually asked to leave the private school I was attending because the headmaster said I was an embarrassment to the school.

"After a few months of Teen AA, I started to think about what my friend had done. She'd saved my life. I really had messed everything up. That's why I moved down here to live with my grandparents. It was really awful; especially the way I treated my friend who really just wanted to help me. Before I moved here, I called her up and went to see her. We both cried for almost two hours. I thanked her a hundred times, and now I call her every night to thank her for what she did. So let me tell you what I think. I think … no, I know, that *if your friend is using drugs or alcohol, you should tell her parents, the school counselor, and the police!*"

Then she broke into big sobs with tears rolling down her face and sat down trembling to a standing ovation from her classmates.

Beth's new friends surrounded her at that point, and I couldn't get close enough to tell her how brave I thought she was. Before I could establish order out of this chaos, the bell rang and the students dispersed, escorting their new heroine out of the room and out of my life. I sat at the desk waiting for the teacher to return, not knowing if I should tell her what had just happened or wait until she heard it through the grapevine. She returned with her usual enthusiasm and stopped in her tracks when she saw me staring into space.

"Were they that bad?" she asked.

"No," I answered. "They were that good!"

Teen Alcoholism

I've thought about what Beth said hundreds of times since that day, and have related the story to many teens. This lesson is one we should all learn because alcohol is no small problem for our school kids and their parents. And even though Beth's problem was alcohol, the same could be said about drugs.

In 2006, alcohol problems alone cost our nation more than $224 billion.[69] As of this writing, "Alcohol-related problems cost every man, woman, and child in the United States $746.00 each year."[70] With a 2012 population of 314,159,000, that equates to more than $234 billion annually. Alcohol is involved in 2006 nearly half the deaths attributed to car accidents, suicides, and homicides—the number one, two, and three causes of death in teenagers.[71] As for drugs, according to recent estimates the total financial cost of drug use disorders to the United States is estimated to be $193 billion annually[72] as well as taking an immeasurable toll on the user's health and general well-being.

Parents significantly underestimate how much alcohol their teens drink. It is estimated that 20 percent of the alcohol consumed in the United States is drunk by minors.[73] A study of 12,352 teenagers in Miami found that 20 percent of them began drinking before the age of 13![74] Too frequently we adults think drinking is only a problem for teenage boys, that girls are somehow resistant to the lure of alcohol. Yet an estimated 4.5 million 12- to 17-year-old girls reported consuming alcohol during the past year. (According to the National Institute on Alcohol Abuse and Alcoholism, 39 percent of ninth-grade girls in 2005 reported drinking in the past month.)

An article in *Girls' Life Magazine* (GL) indicates that "for the first time in history, teen girls drink more than boys. Almost 40 percent of ninth-grade girls have had a drink in the past month versus only 34 percent of boys. And a whopping 45 percent of high school girls drink alcohol."[75]

However, the 2007 National Survey of Drug Use and Health showed that, "[A]mong youths aged 12 to 17, the percentage of males who were current drinkers [had had at least one alcoholic beverage in the past month] (14.2 percent) was similar to the rate for females (15.0 percent)."[76],[77]

The Century Council, a national not-for-profit organization funded by distillers dedicated to fighting drunk and underage driving, commissioned a program called Teenage Research Unlimited and fielded a study of teenage drinking in 2005. The study revealed that although 30 percent of 16- to 18-year-old girls say they drink with friends, only 9 percent of their mothers think their daughters are drinking.[78]

Although adult males are more likely than their female peers to report past-month alcohol use, among 12- to 17-year-olds, the reported rate of past month alcohol use was almost equal with females (17 per-cent for males compared with 18 percent for females). [79]

There's Much A Parent Can Do

As horrid as these statistics sound, there is much a parent can do. According to former Congresswoman

Susan Molinari, chair of The Century Council, "We parents are the most significant influence in [a] teens' decision to drink or not to drink." The mother of two girls, she emphasizes the need for parents to talk with their kids about drinking as well as drug and tobacco use. Parents, she continued, "need to have the conversation early and often."[80]

A new survey of 1,000 American teens ages 12 to 17 conducted by The National Center on Addiction and Substance Abuse at Columbia University (CASA) found the following:

> "[Only] one in four teens in America (27%, about 6.5 million) lives with "hands-on" parents, parents who have established a household culture of rules and expectations for their teen's behavior and monitor what their teens do, such as the television shows they watch, the CDs they buy, what they access on the Internet, and where they are spending evenings and weekends. These teens are at one quarter the risk of smoking, drinking, and using drugs as teens with "hands-off" parents."[81]

That last sentence says it all, but some adults and parents do not take much of a stand against drugs and alcohol. Fred Hechinger in *Fateful Choices*, a book published by the Carnegie Council on Adolescent Development, states:

> "During the 1960s and 1970s, many adults, wanting to be on the youth side of the generation gap, publicly played down the

> harmful effects of drugs, or even urged their acceptance. Unfortunately, such opinions were widely expressed by certain university faculty members, psychologists, and others who had reputations as experts or otherwise commanded the respect of young people. They contradicted those who warned about drugs' potential dangers and sometimes even pressed the matter of drug use as a civil liberties issue. Such misguided voices have largely fallen silent, but their effect lingers."[82]

Adult Responsibility

Some parents mistakenly think that kids will eventually drink, so why not provide them a place to drink safely? I remember Sharon, a girl I saw for her college physical the day after she graduated from high school. When I entered the room she was sitting quietly holding her head in her hands. She was such a pretty girl that it almost distracted me from the reeking smell of alcohol on her breath.

"Don't talk," she said as I entered the room. "I had too much to drink last night and my head is killing me. Can I just go home and we can do this some other time?"

"That's fine with me," I replied, "But you'll have to explain to your folks why we have to reschedule."

"Duh," she replied, inferring I was some kind of dinosaur. "We had a graduation party. They were there."

I was a naïve young doctor just starting my practice and couldn't for the life of me imagine her dad, a professional, allowing an underage daughter to drink to excess at his party. Maybe she's not telling the whole truth, I thought, so I asked, "So your folks had a party and let you have too much to drink?"

She lifted her head from her hands and looked at me through her beautiful but bloodshot, deep brown eyes. She opened her mouth and stared at me, but did not say anything. I'm sure she couldn't believe my incredulous attitude. Finally she said, "The purpose of a graduation party is to get drunk and celebrate. I'm going home."

Fortunately, she did not add "stupid" to the end of the sentence. I followed her to the waiting room where her dad was waiting.

"Dad, I'm sick," she said. "Let's go home and do this some other time." Then she walked out the door.

Dad shrugged his shoulders, smiled, and promised to reschedule. Giving him the benefit of the doubt, I suspect he thought there was nothing he could do to prevent his children from drinking, so he would "keep them safe and let them drink at home." But research suggests otherwise. Alcohol has a toxic effect on the developing brain, and the brain continues to develop until the early 20s. The younger kids start to drink the more permanent is the damage. Most of the damage is to the frontal part of the brain. That's the part which is used to make decision making. That explains why people who start using alcohol at a young age often make poor choices.

Parents exert significant influence on whether their kids choose to drink, smoke, or use illegal drugs.

And the earlier parents talk to kids about their social problems, the more effective they are. The number one reason teens give for not using alcohol, tobacco, or drugs is that they do not want to disappoint their parents.[83]

An interesting study in 2000 from the *Journal of the American Academy of Child and Adolescent Psychiatry* confirms what we discussed in Tools 5 and 6 by noting that religiosity as defined by being affiliated with a religious denomination and having a personal relationship with the Divine was associated with decreased use of alcohol, tobacco, and drugs.[84]

So if you have children, start talking to them at age 10 or 11, or even younger, about alcohol and drugs. Tell them what you expect their behavior to be and bring up the subject again every chance you get. (Hollywood and its stars will provide you with more than enough opportunities.) You might also consider doing what Coach Larsen did (see Tool Number Seven) and be a positive role model. And be sure you and your family are involved in a religious community.

If you or your kids know some teen or preteen who is using alcohol or drugs, remember Beth and do them a favor: tell their parents, the school, and the police. In time, they will thank you.

Parenting Tips

- Discuss with your kids how peer pressure differs from peer permission.
- Don't accept peer permission (even if it is called peer pressure) as an excuse for un-acceptable behavior. Kids really make their own decisions.
- Remember that positive parental pressure is as influential as peer permission or pressure, if not more so.
- Know your kids' friends and their friends' parents.
- Re-evaluate your own friendships. Are your friends the kind of people you want your kids to become? If not, it's time for a change.
- Keep tobacco, alcohol, and drugs out of your home or at least away from your kids!
- Talk with your kids frequently about alcohol, tobacco, and drugs. Use every teachable minute that society provides.
- If you use alcohol, use it with temperance and responsibility. If you use tobacco or illegal drugs, QUIT.
- Encourage your kids to tell the authorities if they know of a peer who is using alcohol, tobacco, or drugs.

Part IV

Habits

People are creatures of habit; we do the things that are "programmed" into our brains. One of the jobs of parents is to help kids develop the habits that will govern them the rest of their lives. It is possible to change habits and you will learn how in this section. But, it is a whole lot easier and better to not develop bad habits in the first place. Here you will meet some incredible kids who will help us understand where both good and bad habits come from, how to develop good ones, and how to get rid of the bad ones.

Tool 9

The "Off" Button

She sat among us, at the best,
A not unfeared, half-welcome guest,
Rebuking with her cultured phrase,
Our homeliness of words and ways. …
She blended in a like degree,
The vixen and the devotee.

—John Greenleaf Whittier

In the fall of 2005, I became aware of a Sunday night television show called "Grey's Anatomy." Having extensively studied the book Gray's Anatomy many years earlier, my curiosity was piqued; so I turned on the "half-welcome guest" most people call a TV.

The show opened with a young glamorous couple bursting into a bedroom in a passionate embrace while he rapidly undressed her and fell on top of her onto a waiting bed. As this scene fortunately faded from view, it was replaced by another beautiful couple similarly embraced and rushing to an open bed while the woman in a passionate fit undressed her mate and they both fell, in prurient pose, onto satin sheets. A third couple competed more successfully as they feverishly undressed each other even more rapidly than either of the first two, but with the same end result. A final passionately entangled couple entered another room as I clicked them into oblivion.

"What on earth was that?" I asked of no one in particular. But my wife, Mary, who had shared the scenes with me replied, "Welcome to Sunday night TV. Get used to it."

"Well," I replied, "I'll have no part of it. Let's see what's on the History Channel."

As the picture came into focus, we saw a group of archeologists digging in what appeared to be a desert or some sand dunes. Then the announcer intoned, "In search of Sodom and Gomorrah."

"What!" I all but shouted at the television. "Stop digging! Both cities are only a few channels away."

After a glare from Mary, I settled down to thinking. What irony, looking for Sodom and Gomorrah when we are practically living there. No need to search the desert for those sinful cities when you can see the same salacious activity every Sunday night on "Desperate Housewives." And what have they done to my Gray's Anatomy?

This Sunday night actually happened, just as I described it! But, that was in 2005, since then things have not improved. Matter of fact, they have become worse, much worse!

I won't go on criticizing this program because I've never seen a whole show. Instead, I want to tell you about a wonderful, thinking teenager who shares some of my views about our "half-welcome guest"— television!

Turning Off the TV

Darrel was a high school junior in the fall of 1999 when I saw him for his annual health evaluation. I have to admit, he was not the brightest kid I ever met. As a matter of fact, he required some special-education classes; but he had a great smile and a magnetic personality. I found him interesting in a subtle way and over the years I grew fond of him.

He came in this day with his dad, as he usually did. Dad, a quiet and pleasant driver for UPS, was still in his "browns." He stood to greet me when I entered the room.

"Good to see you, Doctor," he said folding the morning paper as he extended his hand.

"Darrel needs his 100,000 mile check-up," he joked. "And probably an oil change as well. He's been running with the cross-country team, and I know for sure his wheels need grease."

Darrel blushed at his dad's attempt at truck humor and extended his hand. "Never mind him," he said. "He tries too hard to be funny."

"I understand," I replied. "I have a dad too, you know, and what's more, I am one. So I know how annoying we can be. But just be glad he cares enough to bring you in to see me."

Darrel's evaluation was rather uneventful and we were soon finished. Dad was back in the room and the three of us were casually talking about the tragedy which had just occurred. Columbine was the first of too many mass school shootings. On April 20, 1999, two high school boys brought an arsenal of weapons to a High School in Colorado and shot everyone they could see. They killed 12 students and a teacher and wounded 23 others before they turned the guns on themselves.

While I put Darrel's medical record in order, I said, "Tell me, Darrell, what do you think can be done to prevent things like that from happening again?"

This was a simple question I had asked dozens of kids before and I knew, like everybody else knew, that there was no answer. But Darrel surprised me when he looked first at me and then glared at his dad and said, "*If parents turned off their TVs they could be more involved with their kids' lives.*"

My first reaction was to think Darrel was trying to pick a fight with his dad, and in a way he was. He certainly seemed to have his dander up about this one, something I had not seen in him before as he was usually calm and polite.

"You watch your share," was Dad's only retort.

"Not as much as you do!" Darrel shot back.

"Sure, now, but you used to watch a lot. Before you started school you watched it all day," Dad replied calmly.

"Dad! That was ten years ago and doesn't count. I don't have time to watch now. And you still watch three to four hours each night," Darrel said, anxious to make his point.

But Dad was unshakable. "You're right," he said, acknowledging defeat and ending the discussion at the same time.

Having conquered Dad, Darrel turned to me. "It's true. So many of my friends' dads are just like him. We could all be making bombs in our garages and they wouldn't know until they saw it on the TV. Parents should pay more attention."

Darrel is so right about television (and other screen addictions: gaming and the Internet) interfering with parenting. Most of us are guilty of letting it occupy too much of our time, and time is really all we have to give to our families.

Television and other electronic media have a way of consuming us. According to a Nielson Survey for 2012 teens watch an average of 24 hours of TV each week, not including video games, computer time, or taped programming; grade school kids watch even more. And, parents watch more than 34 hours each week plus 3-6 hours of taped programming.[85] Many dads I know turn the set on for the evening news and sit in their chairs and watch until bedtime.

Time is really all we have to give to our families. I have not found any studies on the effect television has on parenting; all the research seems to be directed to the effect it has on kids, as if adults are not interested in or affected by it at all. But common sense tells us that a parent cannot really interact with a child or learn how his day went or what he and his friends have been up to or help with homework or chores or do any active parenting while watching television. As much as we think we can multi-task, the truth of the matter is, when it comes to parenting, we can't! Kids need and deserve some undivided attention from their parents if they are to successfully learn the skills needed to succeed in life.

Interfering With Life

Television, gaming, and the Internet interfere with more than just parenting. Zach was a 13 y/o boy who was concerned that he watched too much TV. He knew too much screen time, like too much junk food, was not a good thing. During his visit he lamented his association with the tube, particularly.

"I come home from school and want to do my homework or my chores or shoot hoops," he said. "I want to play basketball, so I really need to practice every day. But I can't walk past the TV without turning it on. Then the next thing I know, two or three hours have gone by and I haven't done any of the things I wanted to do. *TV keeps me from doing the things I want to do and should do.*"

"Do you think you're addicted to it?" I asked.

"Nah, I'm not addicted," he said. "It's just that once it's on it's hard to turn it off. Watching is so easy. I don't even have to think, just relax."

"Do you have one in your room?"

"No, Mom won't let me. I just watch in the family room."

"Good for your mom. She probably knows that kids who have a TV in their room are twice as likely to smoke pot, and more likely to drink alcohol or have sex," I said.[86] "And I'm sure you know that watching TV and playing computer games makes you less active, so you gain weight. I can see that's not one of your problems, but it is a very serious concern for many patients. If you ever watch someone watching TV, you will see that they don't move. I like to say that TV turns people into statues; they just sit and stare. Watch them sometime!"

Too Much TV

The problem with television alone cannot be overstated! One-third of all children less than six years of age live in a home where the TV is on almost all the time.[87] Those between eight and thirteen have an incredible six hours a day in front of either a TV or a computer screen![88] By the time a youngster graduates from high school, he will have seen more than 200,000 episodes of violence and witnessed about 8,000 murders.[89] No wonder our society has become immune to the presence of real violence

Even if television had a neutral effect on kids, just think what they could do with all that time. Sadly, adults spend almost as much time watching television as their kids.

An April 2008 study in the *Pediatrics* journal noted that teen boys who have a television in their bedrooms watched more TV, had lower grade point averages, ate less fruit, and had fewer meals with their families than teen boys who did not have a bedroom TV. Likewise with teen girls: the ones with bedroom TVs had lower grade point averages, exercised less, ate fewer vegetables, and participated in fewer family meals.[90]

The American Academy of Pediatrics recommends that teens not have a bedroom TV, but this advice has fallen on deaf ears as the study found that 68 percent of teen boys and 57 percent of teen girls have a TV in their rooms.[91] And an incredible 26 percent of infants under two have a bedroom TV,[92] even though the AAP recommends no TV or video viewing for babies this age.[93] What about infant learning videos like *Brainy Baby* or *Baby Einstein*? A study of 1000 parents and infants from Minnesota and Washington concluded that children who watched these videos were no smarter; as a matter of fact, they had less engagement with others and fewer words in their vocabulary.[94]

A recent editorial in the *Wall Street Journal* noted that parents are failing to police their kids' media consumption.[95] It cited a new study from the Kaiser Family Foundation that found technological additions like DVDs, videos, music, the Internet, computer video games, etc., have resulted in the average eight-to-eighteen-year-old getting 8.5 hours of screen exposure every day. Furthermore, many kids are entertaining themselves in "the privacy of their own bedrooms." That's real trouble.

"The most startling revelation in the Kaiser report is that for a majority of kids there are no rules in the household about media use," the *Journal* reported:

> Where there are rules, often they aren't enforced, or they apply only to how many hours children watch TV, not to what they watch. So what explains the absence of rules and parental supervision? Perhaps it's the huge effort involved. Busy parents have to muster the energy to learn how to use V-chips, ratings systems and computer filtering. They have to make sure that the songs kids download are the

> "radio," or cleaned-up, versions. Maybe some parents are ambivalent about playing the role of censor. Monitoring and enforcing are never-ending tasks.[96]

A Zogby poll in March 2007 found that 79 percent of viewers thought there was too much graphic sex, bad language, and violence on television. Yet 88 percent did not know how to use the V-chip, or knew but hadn't used it.[97] A poll by the Parents Television Council showed that "of shows containing sexual content, 63 percent lack the 'S' descriptor, 42 percent of shows containing violence lack the 'V' descriptor, and 44 percent of shows containing foul language lack the 'L' descriptor."[98] Essentially, despite the good intentions of the ratings system, programs are being rated incorrectly.

The Truth about TV

A lot of today's parents were raised with television—cable television to boot. They think, "Well, look at me. I turned out all right. All this worry about TV viewing is just a bunch of hysteria from experts who don't have anything else to get worked up about." Like other parents, they want what is best for their kids; they believe kids, even infants, can learn by watching TV. But research has documented that even "educational" shows and videos, while they may teach catchy rhymes or even the ABC's, have an overall negative effect on learning.[99] Let's look at the facts.

In reviewing medical literature the past few months, I made a list of some of the possible harmful effects associated with watching too much television:

- Delayed vocabulary acquisition in children ages 8 through 16 months[100]
- Shortened attention span[101]
- Increased risk of Attention Deficit Hyperactivity Disorder[102]
- Sleep problems- trouble going to sleep, increased waking during the night, and increased tiredness during the day, difficulty waking in the morning[103]
- Increased consumption of caffeine[104]
- Increased consumption of snack foods[105]
- Increased fat in diet[106]
- Decreased physical activity[107]
- Obesity[108],[109]
- Increased risk of smoking[110]
- Increased risk of using pot or other drugs[111]
- Increased use of alcohol[112]
- Younger age of initiating sexual activity[113]
- Increased aggressive behavior[114]
- Increased delinquency[115]

Before we go any further, let me point out that it is often very difficult to assign causality just because two things occurred together. However, the above evidence is enough to make parents and doctors concerned that TV viewing contributes to many, if not all, of the above. And, what harm can come from not watching TV?

Certainly a show or two each day may help children and adults relax, but more than that steals valuable time better spent in other activities. Some ask if kids who spend a good deal of time playing video games may develop better manual dexterity and might be faster at learning some of the fine handwork needed to maneuver real life objects such as fighter planes and robotic surgical equipment. This effect has not been established and even if it were, it no way balances the time lost to the pursuit of worthwhile social interactions. Dr. Christakis from Seattle Children's Research Institute states: "No studies to date have demonstrated benefits associated with early infant TV viewing".[116]

Other than David Kleeman, Director of the American Center for Children and Media,[117] and a number of bloggers, I can find no scientific articles showing any real benefits of children watching TV.

Because of the above adverse effects of television viewing, and perhaps other consequences not yet elucidated, the American Academy of Pediatrics has made the following recommendations:[118]

1. Limit children's total media time (screen time) to no more than 1–2 hours of quality programming per day.
2. Remove TV sets from children's bedrooms.
3. No TV for children under 2 years of age.

4. Monitor the shows children and adolescents are viewing.
5. View TV programs along with your children and discuss the content.
6. Use controversial programming as a stepping-off point to initiate discussions about family values, violence, sex, and drugs.
7. Use the videocassette recorder wisely to show or record high-quality, educational programming for children.
8. Support efforts to establish comprehensive media-education programs in schools.
9. Encourage alternative entertainment for children, including reading, athletics, hobbies, and creative play.

Other Ways to Spend Your Time

There are so many alternatives to sitting and watching television, gaming, or surfing the Internet. One winter in Wisconsin we had a week-long ice storm that got many of us thinking. Because the electricity was off for the whole week (and in some homes, for almost two weeks), lives changed. People with gas stoves cooked for their neighbors who had electric, they heated water for those with electric water heaters, and people shared extra blankets and coats. Neighbor helped neighbor.

School was out, the stores were closed, and the state closed the roads into and out of our little town. By some act of fortune, the hospital and our house had underground wires from another community, and we had electricity! The hospital served as an oasis in the storm, housing as many people as could fit inside. The staff used snowmobiles to transport patients. We had extension cords running from our house to our neighbors' to power their furnace fans. Two families of six lived with us for that week. It didn't take long to empty our freezer, but the other families had food thawing in theirs, which they brought over and cooked. We did dishes and laundry all day for seven straight days, but there was always a game of Monopoly, Ping-Pong, or Pit going on somewhere in our crowded house. In short, it was great fun!

It seems everybody in town had a good time in spite of the difficulties. For weeks after, everyone talked about how they played games, did puzzles, and read aloud to each other under candlelight—all because there was no electricity to power TVs. When the lights came on, many families decided to stop their cable service because they realized how much television intruded on their lives, and the fun times continued. But gradually old habits returned, and soon the town folks were watching the tube again and ignoring each other.

It is possible to limit your use of screen media and that of your kids. I often advise teens like Zach, who want to decrease their TV consumption, to make a list of all the shows they would like to watch. Then, pick out their favorite one-hour of TV each school day and two hours for each weekend day to watch, remembering that any computer game time must fit into that same hour. Then they write that TV show in their homework assignment book, cross if off the homework list when it's over, and then turn off the television set. Many families are surprised that this simple act really works.

There are lots of ways to control TV in your home and add some fun to your family's life while you're at it. Try a "Family Game Night" as a useful tool for spending quality time with family members. Plan one night each week to turn off the TV and other electronic media and play games with your family. Make it a priority! Put it on your calendar! Respect that night like you would your bowling night, tennis night, your Bunko night, or Monday Night Football! Your kids—guaranteed—will enjoy it because according to the 2005 Horatio Alger Study of Our Nation's Youth, almost half of our teenagers admit that they want to spend more time with their families.[119]

Wouldn't a game night be a great way to spend that extra time? Think of what kids can learn from playing games. Even preschoolers can learn honesty, counting, color recognition, and waiting in line. As games get more sophisticated, kids learn spelling, math, teamwork, perseverance, patience, good sportsmanship, honesty, strategy, and goal setting. Many games have opportunities to teach how to make choices and to live with the consequences of those choices. Kids can learn many of these things from computer games as well, but relating to a computer and relating to a family member must never be considered equivalent. Kids need time to socialize, and family is the very best place for socialization most importantly, games are fun. They promote togetherness and build the family bond.

When you think of your childhood, do you remember the movies you saw on TV, or the fun you and your family had playing some game or doing something many may even consider foolish? Family Game Night is when memories are built.

An additional benefit is that games provide many opportunities for teaching values to your children. These opportunities are the conversations where values are transferred and where character develops.

Even short and simple games can be fun. Some years ago, our daughter and her family spent the Christmas holidays with us. One evening, before we cleaned up the kitchen, we sat at the table and played "I went on a picnic and I took along . . ." This is a game in which each person around the table adds something in alphabetical order to the picnic basket, and the next person in line has to name all the things in the basket and then add a new item. All the kids, seven to fifteen, and the adults of every age enjoyed the game and each other. "Let's play it again!" Maria, the youngest one, declared. "The next time, we eat." So we did.

But television isn't the only "half-welcome guest" we entertain. How often do we see a young parent driving down the street talking on a cell-phone while the children are in the back watching some video? I contend that travel time can be turned into quality time by talking with the kids, or playing travel games.

Electronic media entertainment is everywhere and involves everyone. At the YMCA recently, I saw an older man listening to his iPod while working out with the free-motion equipment. Somehow he managed to get the wire from the iPod to his ear-bud entangled with the weight machine's cable. I didn't laugh (though I was tempted) as I helped him extract himself from his entertainment.

Every day I see runners and walkers go by my house with their ears plugged with some entertaining, electronic gadget. Just last week my wife and I were out for a walk and saw a woman walking on the other side of the street with two school-age children. I presume they were hers. The boy, who looked to be about 12, was lagging behind the two women, so I called to them, "Hey, he's gaining on you. Don't let him catch you!"

All three of them reached up and extracted their ear-buds. "Pardon?" they said in unison (probably the only thing they had done together all day). Here was an opportunity for some high-quality family time and they were wasting it listening to who knows what.

Take a look around your house and see if you have too many half-welcome guests. Ask yourself if some of them have worn out their welcome and need to be replaced with some quality family time.

Television Viewing and ADD/ADHD

One last note as I think about Darrel. When I first met him he had been diagnosed with ADD (attention deficit disorder). I wondered if all the television he had watched prior to starting school had anything to do with his developing ADD. Recently, researchers in Seattle observed the television viewing habits of over 2,500 youngsters and concluded: "The likelihood of a child being diagnosed with attention deficit disorders increases to 10 percent for those who watched one to two hours [of television daily], 20 percent for those who watched between two and three hours, 30 percent for children glued to the set for three to four hours."[120] From their findings, it is apparent that the problem gets bigger depending on the amount of television being consumed.

Exactly why this happens is not known, but the frequent change of scenes and the rapid sequence of events typical of most TV shows may, in the researchers' opinion, "permanently alter normal brain development."[121] Apparently, studies of newborn rats show that an over-stimulated environment causes the structure of the brain to change. People aren't rats, and we can't always compare laboratory animals with people, but at least this is a start as scientists try to understand ADD.

ADD and ADHD (ADD with hyperactivity) perhaps have multiple causes, including a genetic factor. Likewise, there are many possible treatment options, including family and individual counseling, alternative parenting styles, changes in sleep and bedtime routine, increased exercise, more time out of doors, limited TV, and last of all, drugs.

I do not like using drugs for ADD or ADHD unless the symptoms are extreme and other treatment methods, including behavior modification, have failed. A study reported in May 2005 from Oslo, Norway, concluded:

> "[W]hen the environment supplies clear rules for conduct, immediate and frequent reinforcers and predictable consequences of misconduct, there is no difference between children receiving medication and those not receiving medication."[122]

Often altering the environment by increasing the amount of sleep, decreasing television time, and increasing the amount of time spent outdoors is more beneficial than Ritalin or any other drug.

If problems still exist after making these changes—along with behavior counseling and family therapy—I might consider a medication like Ritalin; but as a rule, I do not like to use stimulants or other psychoactive drugs with children.

Darrel had been on Ritalin for several years when he became my patient, but he did not like the way it made him feel and his Dad did not like what it did to his appetite. "He's skinny enough," Dad protested. Ritalin and other stimulants often cause a dull headache, abdominal pain, and decreased appetite. I was in full agreement with stopping the meds. Since then, Darrel has done as well as he was doing on medication, and graduated with his class the following year.

Many parents and physicians, however, do not agree with me, and the use of drugs for ADD has exploded. Medications used to treat ADHD make up three of the five most frequently prescribed drugs for American children. According to the Agency for Healthcare Research and Quality, more than $1.3 billion was spent on these drugs in 2004, the last year data was available.[123] Unfortunately, many parents and doctors find giving a pill easier and quicker than making the lifestyle changes needed to help these kids.

Results of a study published in the May 2009 issue of *Pediatrics* disagrees with me. In a six-year retrospective study, investigators found that the use of medication resulted in a net gain of 0.19–0.29 school years. According to their estimates, these medications cost $2.2 billion per year. When the best a year of treatment with medications can do is a week in school at a cost of billions of dollars, perhaps we need to be cautious about how much these medications really help.[124]

I know that television and other screen media are here to stay, and I can't control what is broadcast or who watches what. But I also know that I can control what I watch, and parents can and should control what they and their children view. If there is not enough evidence out there to condemn most television shows today, Darrel and Zach gave us two more good reasons to use discretion in what we watch. We should listen to our kids, find the off button and use it regularly.

Tool 10

Be Happy, Positive, and Nice

The real world is not easy to live in. It is rough; it is slippery. Without the most clear-eyed adjustments we fall and get crushed.

—Clarence Shepard Day

Yesterday I read a column about attitude by a motivation speaker who started his career while in college selling books door-to-door. He said he wishes he would have know what attitude really was when he was 21. Don't we all? The following stories illustrate how some young people used good attitudes to make life better for themselves and others.

The 1979 award-winning movie *Breaking Away* (1979) won an Oscar for screenwriter Steve Tesich, and those who saw it were endeared to the teenage boy who wanted to be Italian. In the film, bicyclist Dave Stoller becomes enamored with the Cinzano racing team from Italy and spends the summer training and "becoming" Italian. He studies Italian, eats Italian food, listens to Rossini and Italian opera, and, much to his dad's chagrin, shaves his legs to emulate the foreign racers. When he meets a college girl, he pretends to be an Italian exchange student to impress her. The filming and screen writing were great, but what impressed me most was Dave's total commitment to becoming something he wasn't—Italian.

The desire to change, to become something they aren't (i.e., adults) is what all kids do. And it's what parents, teachers, coaches, and yes, even doctors, are supposed to help them do. For some, it's not an easy task; others seem to zoom into adulthood without the slightest hint of a problem. Many books have been written about the transition trying to explain the plethora of problems that can occur and how to avoid and treat them. Among these authors, Drs. James Dobson, Frank Pittman, David Elkind, and William Pollack come readily to mind; but 17-year-old Eric had an easier solution.

Becoming Who You Pretend to Be

I had seen Eric because of infectious mononucleosis (mono) during his junior year in high school. He was a talented basketball player, but his illness forced him to settle for a shortened season. I looked forward to seeing how well he would do his senior year, as did his coach and fellow students. He had many fans and friends because he was so much more than a basketball player; he was a student leader with a great attitude, and he was about to teach me a valuable lesson.

Early in his senior year he came to see me for his physical. When I entered the exam room he smiled, showing off dazzling white teeth. He rose to shake my hand and introduce his mother.

"Hi, Doctor." Then gesturing to his mom he added, "I don't think you two have met. Dad always came with me before. This is my mother, Shirley."

Mother smiled with pride as she offered me her hand. "So nice to see you," she said, and then added, "Eric and his dad have told me so much about you. It is a pleasure to finally meet you."

We engaged in a bit of social chatter, reviewed Eric's health, and in due time, Mom retired to the lobby while Eric and I proceeded with his evaluation, which was un-remarkable. As we finished I said, "Eric, you seem to be an outstanding young man. I'd be proud to have a son like you."

He thanked me and I asked him one of my pet questions. "Tell me, Eric, how would you like to have a son like you?"

"Like I am? Or, like I pretend to be?" he asked.

"Is there a difference?"

"Yes," he replied. "I sometimes get down and negative, but I try to be happy, optimistic, and positive because I know if you try, *you will become the man you pretend to be*."

"Become the man you pretend to be," I echoed. "What an outstanding concept. And as I think about it, it really is what happens, isn't it?"

"One of my friends says, 'Fake it until you make it,' but I like the way I said it better. It sounds more optimistic. Don't you agree?" he asked.

"You will become the man you pretend to be." I sure do. How did you come up with this … can I call it a philosophy?"

"I guess it is a philosophy, isn't it?" he answered. "I've never called it that. I just think of it as a way to become a better person. It started when I was in a school play in the seventh grade. I found out the more I acted like the character in the play, the more I became him. I wanted to be a good basketball player, too, so I thought, why not act like a good basketball player? So I did. Then Coach noticed I had more confidence, and he started to play me more, and that's how it started. Then in youth group we always talked about becoming better, and I thought if it works for basketball it should work for other stuff, too. I don't want to brag, and I'm not as good a person as I should be, but I keep on trying."

"Well, Eric, I think you're doing super!" I said. "Your philosophy is so great I want to tell other kids about it. Is that okay with you?"

"What do you mean?" he asked.

"Well, I see a lot of kids who have problems to overcome or who need to make some changes in their lives, and I think it may be helpful to tell them what you said about becoming the man you pretend to be. I wouldn't tell them it's your motto unless you want me to. What do you think?"

"Do it if you think it will help someone," Eric replied. "I know it helps my day go better."

Eric and I talked a bit more about his motto, how it relates to improving one's life, and how it might help the transition from childhood to adulthood. Soon, his mom was back in the exam room and I told her how privileged I felt to be able to see and care for Eric. I asked him to discuss his philosophy with her on the way home.

Eric had a great senior basketball season and went on to play NCAA Division II college ball; I went on using his wisdom with my other patients.

The Power of the Positive

Eric's idea is not new, nor is it rare. It's just that I had never heard it expressed like that before. There's an old song from the late 1950s, "Pretend," whose lyrics suggest, "Pretend you're happy when you're blue." The songwriter knew that by pretending, you could become what you want to be.

In C.S. Lewis's *Screwtape Letters*, the devil (Screwtape) says, "All mortals tend to turn into the thing they are pretending to be."[125] Screwtape was a lead devil teaching his devil nephew how to gain control of a man. He was, of course, talking about bad habits, but the same can surely be said about developing good habits.

Recently I attended a Boy Scout Honor Court where a friend's son was being honored as a new Eagle Scout. There I was reminded that Boy Scouts are "Trustworthy, Loyal, Helpful, Friendly, Courteous, Kind, Obedient, Cheerful, Thrifty, Brave, Clean, and Reverent." I wondered if they really are all these things, or are they becoming all these things by pretending? Aren't they just rehearsing for the future?

Many might call the Scouts egotistical for confessing such virtues, thinking they are just daydreaming or lying to themselves; but professional motivators and coaches call that "visualizing success." Visualizing success causes the brain to believe we are already successful; and this subconscious belief gives us the confidence we need to be comfortable with success. It removes the fear of failure. As we continue to visualize the future and our place in it, our brain gives us positive feedback that prepares us for victory. In short, envision the future, plan for it, execute the plan, and enjoy the success.

Good basketball coaches tell their players to stand on the free-throw line and visualize the ball rising from your hands and dropping—swish— through the net.

Jack Nicklaus, probably the world's greatest golfer prior to the advent of Tiger Woods, says in his book *Golf My Way* that before every shot he "sees" the shot in his mind. "First, I 'see' the ball where I want it to finish. … Then the scene changes and I 'see' the ball going there: its path, trajectory, and shape, even its behavior on landing. … The next scene shows me making the kind of swing that will turn the previous images into reality."[126]

In addition to pretending, Eric also mentioned maintaining a positive attitude. Psychologist Donald Clifton said,

"Studies show that organizational leaders who share positive emotions have workgroups with a more positive mood-enhanced job satisfaction, greater engagement and improved group performance."[127]

Isn't that what all employers are looking for in their employees? And don't parents desire something similar for their "workgroup"— their kids? Parents who agree should try to develop positive attitudes and become the parents they know their kids need. We should listen to Eric and visualize ourselves as fulfilling the role of great parents. Then we will have the strength to make a plan to become who we want to be. It is no secret that kids' attitudes are learned from their parents. Parents with an "I can" attitude have children who know their accomplishments can be just short of limitless.[128]

Have More Fun

I'll never forget the lesson I learned from an 11-year-old boy on the ski hill many years ago. We were standing in the lift line when a fellow skier asked him if he was having fun. He assured all of us within ear-shot that he was having a great time. Then the stranger asked, "Did you have any falls?"

"Yep," the boy replied, "and I had fourteen get-ups today."

"Get-ups?" the man questioned. "What is a get-up?"

The 11 year old philosopher looked at him incredulously. "A get-up is what you do when you fall down. Falls don't count, get-ups do!"

We all fall, but it's what we do after we fall that's important. Remember to get up!

A very interesting 2001 study reported in the *Journal of Personality and Social Psychology* looked at longevity in 180 Catholic nuns, ages 75 to 90, who, in their early twenties, had handwritten short autobiographies. The researchers found that the nuns who reported more positive emotions in their early bios lived an average of ten years longer than those with few positive emotions. It would seem that a negative attitude is worse than smoking, which shortens the life of a smoker by up to seven years. Now I'm not suggesting that it's better to smoke than to be negative, but it does show the value of a positive attitude. A good attitude is a valuable predictor of longevity.

Visualizing the Positive

Some months after Eric's visit, I was talking with 14-year-old Connor about his health habits. It was the first time I had seen Connor. Mom was in the room as I was explaining how important good health habits are. "The habits you make in junior high and high school will determine how well and how long you will live," I said. And then, before I could ask him if he could think of any habits that would help make him healthy, he interjected: "What you're saying is, *boys make the habits and the habits make the man*, right?"

"Right," I replied, impressed. "Can you tell me more?"

"Nah, it's just what my dad tells me all the time. He's right, too, isn't he?"

I wish you could have seen his mother's smile. It was like a jet stream across the sky. This was Connor's moment and she just wanted to enjoy it, realizing what a great father she had picked for her son.

As Connor and his mom left the office, I got to thinking more about habits. Good habits—exercising, healthful eating, adequate sleep, reading, limiting TV, going to church, being optimistic, being happy—are all habits we make while we're young. So, too, bad habits—smoking, drinking, illicit drug use, deceitfulness, pessimism, disrespect for authority, promiscuous sexual activity, unnecessary risk-taking, and aggressive behavior, to name only a few—are ingrained in us before we ever become adults. That's why the teen years are so important in one's life. Too bad so many parents (and society in general) don't understand how important this period of development is.

For a number of years, I taught in medical school. Each year about the beginning of the second semester, many third-year medical students would tell me, "Most of the diseases and problems we see are brought on by the patient."

"Yes," I told them all. "Things haven't changed much since I was in school. We have learned that cervical cancer is almost always a sexually transmitted disease, and now people are giving themselves AIDS; we didn't have that disease when I was a student. But you're right; many of the diseases we see are self-induced." Consider that lung cancer, chronic sinusitis, and bronchitis can all be caused by smoking; and alcohol is responsible for many marital conflicts as well as depression, suicide, cirrhosis, and a host of other physical and emotional diseases. Sexually transmitted diseases, many cases of infertility, cervical cancer, throat cancer, and even adult onset diabetes are a few others that come to mind as being caused by bad habits learned in adolescence or before.

But the good news is that habits can be changed. It is not necessarily easy to change a habit, but it can be done. The secret is to visualize yourself without the old habit and with a new habit to replace it. Then make a plan to think like and act like the person you want to be!

Visualizing our new selves is probably the most important factor in making new habits. That is one of the reasons people who are trying to lose weight put a picture of a thin person on their refrigerator. It helps them visualize themselves as thin and boosts their confidence in their ability to stay on a weight-loss diet.

Forming New Habits

Ian Newby-Clark, an associate professor of psychology at the University of Guelph in Ontario, Canada, who studies habit change, claims there are five steps to forming a new habit.[129]

Work on One Habit at a Time. If you work on changing more than one habit at a time, you run a serious risk of overwhelming yourself and changing no habits at all.

Create a your plan. Write it down, and be as specific as possible. Know what you want to do. Visualize it!

Refine Your Plan. Ask yourself, is your plan realistic? Lay your plan aside for a day or two and come back to it with fresh eyes. Ask a friend to review it to be sure it is a doable project and not pie-in-the-sky.

Make Mini-Plans. Once your plan is as good as you can make it, break it down into steps or mini-plans.

Repeat! Repeat! Repeat! Repeat your behavior until it is automatic.

It usually takes about three weeks of repetitive behavior to develop a new habit or change an old one. If the habit has been around a long, long time, it may take more repetitions and more time, but persistence pays off and in time, even if there are relapses, the new habit can overcome the old. Many habits are so difficult that it takes much longer to develop them. Just think of how long it takes to become an accomplished musician. The many hours of daily practice soon become weeks of practice, months of practice, and then years of practice. To the virtuoso, practice becomes a habit, a way of life!

Letting Go of Bad Habits

Some of us have a few habits that need to be changed; others have many. We all have room in our lives to become better, to improve our health, to change our way of life. And we can do so by consistently making good choices until we have developed the habit to overcome our past behavior. Whatever our age, we all need to periodically review our health habits; our lives depend on them.

Sometimes developing new habits is, in reality, changing an entire life style. Often, we are forced to change our lives against our will. We might develop a chronic disease, lose a loved one, or move to a new home. How we adapt to these changes will depend more on what is inside of us than on what is happening around us. When adjusting to change, our attitude is always more important than the physical problem.

A patient of mine named Blake knew about bad habits and the need for change. He was representative of the kind of teenager every negative TV news story and movie about young people gone wild exploited. His dad was a pediatric surgeon who had recently moved from Arizona in order to be closer to his extended family and to get help for Blake.

When I entered the exam room, Blake was sitting on the exam table with his head in his hands staring at the floor. I extended my hand to Blake and waited a long second until he took it and gave it a weak squeeze. I did not release my grip until he looked me in the eye. Then I tightened it a bit, smiled, and said, "So nice to meet you. I'm sorry you had to come in on such a beautiful day."

I asked Blake to move off the table and onto the chair beside me. After a bit of small talk, I asked him and his dad about his past history, completed the exam, and began to inquire about his health habits.

"Blake," I began, "I have a few dozen questions I ask all the kids to see what kind of health habits they're developing. This is how we determine if you're going to live to be a hundred or if I should call 911 right now. Some of the questions are interesting, some are a bit embarrassing, and some may seem dumb, but they are all important. And remember, unless I think you're in grave danger, all your answers are confidential. Should we get started?"

"Okay, but let me tell you, I have had some bad habits and some good ones," Blake answered. "I'm trying to get rid of the bad ones, so don't be too hard on me!"

"Oh, I'm not here to lecture, judge, or punish your behavior," I assured him. "My job is to help you overcome the bad habits and reinforce the good ones. Since you're my patient, I feel we're in this thing together. Besides, I'm too much of a pushover to be a parole officer."

We laughed together and much too soon we were finished, but not until we talked about how he might turn things around in his life. Then I said, "Let me say I really enjoyed talking with you. Looks like you have tried to get your life back in order and do the right thing. Everybody has done things they aren't proud of, you know. Don't let it get you down. Move on, as they say."

And then I looked him in the eye and said, "If you were my son, I would be proud of you!"

"Really?" he asked in surprise. "If I had a son like me I wouldn't be proud of him." He didn't smile when he said it.

"Hey, I told you I was an old softie; but look, I'm not proud of everything you ever did, I'm not even proud of everything I ever did," I replied, making my case to a teen who had obviously beaten himself down about his conduct as much as others had.

"People make mistakes. People also stop making mistakes. I'm proud that you realized what mistakes you were making and are willing to change your life. That would make any dad proud! Just remember, don't try to change too many things at one time. Adjustment isn't that easy, you know."

"Boy, I know that," Blake said. "First I had to adjust to high school, then we moved and I had to adjust to another school. I got in trouble and had to adjust to life in the lock up. I had to adjust to moving to an apartment in Georgia, then we moved to a house and I had to adjust to a new neighborhood. It seems like *life is just one adjustment after the other*. Then he thought a while, smiled, and said, "Maybe we should all be chiropractors and learn how to adjust!"

We both laughed out loud. His use of wit softened the punch after acknowledging one of the sad facts of life: the only thing we can count on is change! But change was a sore point for Blake, and I realized he needed to talk to someone about it.

We discussed the changes that took place in Blake's past and the changes he needed to make in his life habits. When his father came in to take him home, I took the opportunity to tell him what a fine boy I thought he had. "The three of us," I told him, "with the help of Blake's new counselor, just need to play Michelangelo and chip away the excess stone. So let the chips fly.

"Let me add, I really enjoyed meeting your son. He has a lot going for him, and he'll do fine. You can be proud of him! I sure am."

The Value of Sincere Praise

I wondered how long it had been since someone had told Blake he was proud of him, despite his troubles. Or when was the last time someone gave him a compliment. Honest compliments and other affirmations are so important in how we see ourselves, how we see others and how we react to and with others, and how successful we are in life. A world-wide study[130] of over four million employees at more than 10,000 businesses found that individuals who receive consistent recognition and praise:

- increase productivity,
- improve relationships with co-workers,
- change jobs less often,
- are better liked by customers,
- have fewer injuries on the job.

Build A Positive Attitude

To emphasize the strength and value of affirmation, I have two bags of beans in my office desk drawer: one of white beans and one of red beans. I give five of each to any patient who seems too negative and wants to improve his or her attitude and ask them to place the beans in the right front pocket of their pants.

I instruct them to take out one bean each time they put a hand into that pocket. If the bean is white, they are to find something they like about the person they are with: their looks, their hair, their jewelry, something they're wearing, something they just said, or anything else they like, and give that person a sincere compliment. If they are by themselves, they are to find someone to compliment.

If the bean is red, they are to think of something they like about themselves; and if they are alone, they should voice the self-compliment out loud. If others are present, it is enough to just think about the compliment and smile. In any case, after they give a sincere compliment, they place the bean in their left pocket.

The goal is to move all the beans from the right to the left pocket each day. When they accomplish that, I give them more beans. Kids who follow this program change their observation of others; their impression of themselves and others; and in a few short weeks, their attitudes as well.

This program works for several reasons: when we give someone a sincere, heartfelt compliment, the recipient will usually smile and often return the compliment. After receiving two or three compliments, most people will start to notice the admirer, look forward to seeing him or her again, and soon endear themselves to the individual. When we compliment ourselves, we start to realize that we, too, have value. It is important to remember, however, that we must avoid insincerity at all costs. People, especially teenagers, see through false compliments immediately.

Blake displayed an almost despairing attitude; he was not proud of what he had done and not proud of himself. No one, it seems, not even himself, had ever given nod to anything positive about Blake. It's no wonder he needed to use drugs and delinquent behavior to boost his status. He was just the kind of "good kid" who would join a gang and we would all wonder why.

What Blake needed more than anything else was someone to believe in him; someone who believed, like John Locke, that "the sooner you treat [your son] as a man, the sooner he will begin to be one."[131] Someone needed to find the good inside of Blake and nourish it with sincere compliments and affirmations until he knew he was a valuable human being. Like all of us social beings, he needed someone to help him change.

Choosing Happiness

When we are faced with change there are several tacks we can take. We can deny it, we can fight it, we can accept it, or we can embrace it. If the change is unexpected and unwanted, we may progress through all of these stages—from denial to embracing—with difficulty. Our actions will parallel Dr. Kubler-Ross's stages of grief.[132] Her description (as it relates to change) can be paraphrased as follows: denial of the impending event, bargaining with God or whoever is responsible for the event, becoming angry over the event, becoming depressed, and finally, arriving at resolution and acceptance.

To facilitate change in our lifestyle, it helps to focus first on the good things that may come with change, and try to keep our minds off the negatives. Then by visualizing our new life as better, we will have the energy needed to overcome the anger resulting from a change in our status quo. Most changes in our life turn out to be improvements if we look at them objectively. As we change, we discover that adjusting can be fun. Ben Hogan said, "One of the reasons golf is so fascinating is that the adjustments are endless."[133] So it is with life.

I saw Blake several more times during his last two years of high school. He had some problems with curfew and he met some friends who once helped him get marijuana—but only once. He didn't let a failure get him off tract because he really wanted to change his life, and he had enough character to bounce back. By the time he graduated, he was drug free and ready to adjust to college.

I think of Blake often as I deal with life's changes: retirement, new friends, new town, new store, new church, new home, painful shoulder, painful back, sick grandchild, war, 9/11, Sandy Hook shooting, taxes—the list is endless. But I try to remember what he said: "Life is just one adjustment after another." If we can enjoy the adjustments, our lives will be enriched and we'll be happier. After all, being happy is a habit. As Abraham Lincoln said, "People are just as happy as they make up their minds to be."[134] Take an hour or two and watch *Breaking Away* and do as Dave did: decide to be happy.

When I was in high school, Mrs. Shaw, my English teacher, said "nice" was an overworked word. "It is so over-used," she said, "that it no longer has meaning. Don't use it." But dictionaries define "nice" as fastidious, refined, delicate, precise, subtle, calling for care, tactful, pleasant, attractive, kind, good, or as a general term of approval. What could be wrong with using a word like that? Aren't those characteristics we all would like to possess? And if someone does possess them, shouldn't they be recognized? Yet for the past half-century, every time I say "nice" or write "nice," I hear Mrs. Shaw admonishing, "Don't use it!"

Bennett had a different idea. One beautiful Sunday afternoon he, his dad, and I had agreed to play nine holes of golf. But as luck would have it, Dad couldn't make it; so 17-year-old Bennett and I went on without him.

Try to Be Nice

I didn't know Bennett very well. I sang in the church choir with his dad and frequently met Bennett and his mother after Sunday service. He was short; had a round face with small round, brown eyes; and looked more like 13 than 17. His short hair reminded me of the military recruits I had cared for in the past. He was always pleasant. He shook my hand and greeted my wife and me every time we met; but he remained quiet, talking only if we spoke first.

I enjoyed playing golf with this young man, even though he was beating me. Well, let me be honest—he was annihilating me! We had some great conversations. I learned he had two older brothers, was born in Germany, and had spent a couple of years at a boarding school: his dad's alma mater. He was not exactly crazy about school; he wanted to be a chef. He said he had had a few arguments, but had never been in a fight.

As we approached the ninth tee box, I was sorry we were about to finish. (Sorry, too, that he was beating me.) After I hit my tee shot into the lake, Bennett said in sympathy, "Why don't you just take a Mulligan?" To a non-golfer, that means just take another try; we won't count the first one.

"Thanks, Bennett," I responded. "But I think I'll take my penalty and drop down by the lake. I can probably get on the green from there. Besides, you've beaten me badly today, and I should let the score show that."

"Thanks," he answered as he blushed. "I guess I just feel bad beating you when you invited me to play. Next time you'll probably kick my behind."

"Bennett," I said, "you're just too much. Are you always this kind?"

"Not really," he answered.

"Well, you seem like a pretty great guy to me."

"I'm no Mother Theresa," he responded enjoying the compliment, "but I *try to be nice*."

"You do a great job of it."

We finished the hole, said good-bye, and I thought no more about it until a few days later when I read an article in the local paper about Dolly Parton. One of her past agents was quoted as saying "Dolly is always so nice. She is just wonderful to everybody." Then I started to think. Bill Clinton, regardless of what you thought of him as a politician, was said to be "nice" to everybody. He was the "man" at every party. He made sure everybody around him had a good time. The late Tim Russert was reported as being nice. If you had watched his shows, you would never have seen him insult a guest or confront them in a mean way.

I always start my day with the comics, and my favorite is "Red and Rover." Cartoonist Brian Basset has captured the innocence and imagination of childhood and managed to avoid any meanness. Red is always nice, as is his dog Rover. They're a great pair and they warm my heart at every breakfast. I like Snoopy too, but Lucy can be mean!

Bill Murray in *Groundhog Day* (1993) plays the role of a very wacky, self-centered, miserable weatherman who by some unexplained quirk of nature is forced to live the same Groundhog Day over and over again. After the first few reruns of the same day in Punxsutawney, Pennsylvania, Murray becomes frightened, even suicidal. Even after killing himself, the alarm clock rings, he's back in his hotel bed, and Groundhog Day starts again. Then, as he realizes only he knows the days are reruns, and because he knows what will happen next, he tries to take advantage of people. That doesn't work either; he's still unhappy. But, gradually, his attitude changes. He saves a boy's life, takes piano lessons, and gives to his colleagues and the community. He becomes more concerned about other people than about himself, and all these changes make him happy. When he becomes totally unselfish, loving, and "nice," his alarm rings and it is February 3; Groundhog Day is finally over and Bill Murray awakes a new man. What a story! What a lesson!

But *Groundhog Day* was fiction. Does being nice really make a difference? Can real people be nice, and successful, too?

Being Remembered for Being Nice

Bart Starr was perhaps the greatest quarterback of all time. I know many give this honor to Peyton Manning or Tom Brady, but to us old Packer fans, even Brett Favre is in second place. Starr was the Packers seventeenth-round draft pick in 1956 and played fifteen seasons, leaving the team in 1971. He won six Western Division Titles, five NFL Championships, Super Bowls I and II, and was named MVP for both those bowl games. He went on to coach the Packers from 1975–83, and he earned induction into the Pro Football Hall of Fame in 1977. And he was known as a nice guy.

My son Rafe tells a couple of stories that show just how nice a guy Starr really was. Rafe lived in Kansas City and Bart Starr was there at the opening of a sporting goods store to sign autographs. The lines were long and when Rafe finally got to the counter with Starr, he was surprised to see Bart standing, not sitting, while signing various items the patrons had brought for his signature.

"To whom shall I address this?" Starr asked Rafe.

"My son Harrison," Rafe replied. Then, while Bart was writing, Rafe asked, "Do you have to just stand here? Can't they find a chair for you to sit down?"

"They could," Bart replied, "but I told them if people have to stand and wait to see me, the least I can do is stand to greet them. Seems fair, doesn't it?"

"I guess it does at that," Rafe answered. "And thanks for signing this picture. It will have a place of honor in my son's room." And it does.

Another luminary noted for being nice was former President Jimmy Carter. In fact, he was affectionately known as "Mr. Nice Guy." Mike Nizza in an October 3, 2007, article for *The New York Times* wrote, "Jimmy Carter's nice-guy image has always been a reason to like him, loathe him or laugh at him. ..." Then he went on to tell how the President stood up to a local security chief during his visit to the Darfur region of Sudan when he was told he could not visit a tribal leader in Kabkabiya. He ended the article stating, "In the end, the dispute was resolved in Mr. Carter's usual Nobel-peace-prize style: First a cessation of yelling, and then a compromise. The tribal leader he planned to meet came to him, and they drove off together...."

A final example of being "nice" involves my college roommate's mother, Grace. Grace was refined, delicate, pleasant, attractive, kind, and good. In short, she was all the things dictionaries say "nice" should be. When she talked with you she looked at you, and only at you; you knew she was sincerely interested in what you were saying. When you were with Grace you always felt special. Grace sent many care packages to Rod while he was in school, always with a note to be sure to share with his friends. And Rod had a lot of friends because he was so much like his mother. Rod's intelligence, his determination, and his perseverance made him an oral surgeon; and his kindness (niceness) helped him to become successful as a surgeon and as a colonel in the U.S. Air Force. I was blessed to have such a nice roommate.

When I married, Mary met Grace; she loved her immediately, probably because they are very much alike. Mary has done a wonderful job of being nice. I appreciate it every day.

Nice and Successful

Patrick Steffen, assistant professor of clinical psychology at Brigham Young University, reported in the December 2005 issue of *Annals of Behavioral Medicine* that students with compassion enjoyed better health than those without such an attribute. He defined compassion as "being moved by the suffering of others and having the desire to alleviate that suffering."[135] Since compassion is a part of being nice, Steffen has provided a scientific reason for listening to Bennett.

There's even a book about being nice: *The Power of Being Nice: How to Conquer the Business World With Kindness*, by Linda Kaplan Thaler and Robin Koval. In it they say, "It is often the small kindnesses—the smiles, gestures, compliments, favors—that make our day and can even change our lives."[136]

Do-gooders (nice people) "are the glue that holds offices together."[137] We have all experienced that type of person in our workplaces, but there is a difference between being nice and being a wimpy, passive Milquetoast. Thaler and Koval state, "Nice is not naïve. Nice does not mean smiling blandly while others walk all over you. It is valuing niceness—in yourself and in others—the same way you respect intelligence, beauty, or talent" [138] Like nice co-workers at the office, nice parents are the glue that holds families together. Shouldn't we all have a mission, like Bennett, to try to be nice?

I began to wonder how much being nice has to do with success, so I talked with my neighbor Don who is considered one of the nicest guys on the golf course. Yet I know that he can be firm, too. Don retired as CFO from one of the Fortune 500 companies, so I know he was successful.

"Tell me, Don," I began, "What is the relationship between being nice and being successful in corporate America? Is it true that nice guys finish last?"

"Par, that's a complicated question," Don answered. "Fortunately, I had a lot of good people working for me and with me." (Why is it that successful people always mention first the good people who worked for them? I think it says something about the "good people's" boss.)

Don continued. "Sure, people who are too nice can get run over, but I don't think that's so much about being nice as it is about being weak. Nice, Par, is a difficult word to define. I think," he added, "it has to do with knowing the company's goals and staying focused on those goals and being nice to those who are committed to those goals. You can be nice to those who are not committed by helping them understand the goals or letting them find other work. The mean, egotistical boss seldom succeeds."

I thought nice guys finished last! I was wrong. So why not try to be nice? What can it hurt? Why not listen to Bennett? He showed me how to play golf, he showed me how to be nice, and then he let me in on his personal philosophy. And what a great philosophy it is: Try to be nice!

Parenting Tips

- Know the American Academy of Pediatrics' guidelines for TV watching and abide by them. Never put a TV in a child's or teen's room.
- Do not allow TV, iPods or MP3 players during family time, including mealtime. Use this time to talk with your kids.
- If your child has signs of ADD or ADHD, stop all TV, increase physical activity (preferably out of doors), and seek parenting guidance before ever agreeing to the use of medication
- Decide to be happy! Be positive; throw out the negative.
- Laugh! Share humor with your kids.
- Learn to adjust to the difficulties that may come into your life. Be open to change, welcome it, and do not fear the unknown.
- Be lavish with sincere praise.
- Review your health and your living habits. Change those that are harmful to you and your family.
- Be nice, especially to the people who mean the most to you—your family.
- Be nice to everyone, whether they can do you good or not. It is a sign of real character.

Part V

Economics

Too often we parents try to make everything easy for our kids; we don't want them to have to work too hard. This unit begins with a boy with a different and perhaps better idea. Likewise, many of us grew up thinking that poor was holy. Yet the teens will tell us differently. They know the value of saving, giving and spending money. Listen to them!

Tool 11

Work

The things, Good Lord, that we pray for, give us the grace to work for.

—Thomas More, c. 1510

One of the great privileges I had in my career was being the physician for various sport teams. I spent nine years with a public high school in the little town of Hartford, Wisconsin, and followed that with four years at a private religious high school in Milwaukee. During those years, I met hundreds of outstanding high school athletes; outstanding not so much as athletes, but as people. You can watch college football or NFL ball, but unless you have been involved with the enthusiasm, the dedication, the drama, and the emotion of high school competition, you have not really seen or enjoyed sports. The enthusiasm and dedication I speak of is not limited to the players: the coaches share, and perhaps generate, this emotion. It all reaches a peak on Friday nights on the football field, and that's where I started every autumn weekend for thirteen years.

During the course of those years, I learned that sports really do make life more exciting, more interesting, and a whole lot better. Athletes learn discipline, perseverance, and honesty. They learn how to live with disappointment and how to handle success; they learn the value of preparation, goal setting, and the importance of exercise and a good diet. In short, sports teach character. In spite of evidence to the contrary from some professional athletes, high school athletes really care about their health, their school, and their sport. I love what sports do for high school kids.

Dennis's Story

Dennis was a wide receiver I met during his sophomore year. He was attending a religious high school in Milwaukee on scholarship. I saw him for the first time when I gave a talk to the team on nutrition and hygiene. As one of only two black kids on the team, he stuck out from most of the other players. He also stuck out in one of the first games of the season when he snatched a ball out of the hands of a receiver and sprinted thirty-five yards for the team's first touchdown. It wouldn't be his last.

Several weeks later, his coach brought him into my office with an authorization note from his mother to treat an infection on his leg.

"I told his mom you would call her after you saw him," Coach began. "I hope that's okay. Dennis doesn't have a regular doctor, but he needs to get that leg taken care of before it falls off. I told him you would probably need to amputate it," he finished with a laugh.

I shook Dennis' hand and noted that his smile was only half the intensity of what he had worn during my brief encounters with him and the team.

"Don't worry, Dennis," I said to reassure them both. "We should be able to get you fixed up in time for Friday's game, and we definitely won't need to amputate. Heck, I want to see another pick like you made in three weeks ago. You make the game look easy. But first, why don't you tell me how you hurt your leg."

The forced smile on Dennis's face disappeared as he glanced at the coach. "It's okay," Coach said. "Tell him how it happened."

Dennis took a deep breath, exhaled briskly, and began. "Well, Coach knows that my mom, my sister, and I live alone and that she's a single mother. But nobody knows that I've never seen my dad." Then he turned to the coach and added, "Please don't tell the team, Coach, because they would all laugh and make me feel like I don't fit in, and I feel that way enough of the time already."

"Anyhow," Dennis continued. "We live in a not very nice part of town; it's all we can afford. I have a job in the summer, but Mom won't let me work very much during the school year. I agree with her; I need the time to study. My high school is hard, you know?" He rubbed his hand over his forehead and through his curly, black hair, and sighed.

Why is he telling me this stuff? I wondered. But I'd learned over the years that when my office door closes, any subject is game—relevant or not. In any case, it sounded like he really needed someone to listen to him.

"You're right about that," I agreed. "But what happened to your leg?" I felt I had to get going, even though I really wanted to hear the rest of his story. Perhaps, I could have him come back some time and tell me all the other stuff.

"I'm getting to that," he said, not noticing I was running short on patience. "You see, Saturday afternoon I was shooting hoops with some of my neighbor friends and I fell and scraped my leg in the dirt. When I got home I knew I should have showered and washed it like you said in your talk at school, but it was really cold and ..." He was quiet again, and then continued, mumbling. "We don't have hot water in our apartment, and the landlord hasn't turned the heat on yet." Then he exhaled and in a more moderate voice added, "He says heat costs a lot, and I guess it does."

I nodded in agreement, too numb to talk.

"So by the time I got to shower after practice last night, I guess it was too late and my leg really swelled up. Now it looks like this."

I was pretty sure I could take care of his leg infection—unless it was the virulent staph I had talked about at that high school lecture. Many who play sports contact and spread what we call MRSA (methicillin resistant staph aureus) which can cause minor skin infections or boils and occasionally more serious, even fatal, infections. That's why I am so insistent that all players shower at school right after practice or games and any other time they break open their skin. If an athlete waits until he gets home to shower, other activities like phone calls, computer game, dinner, or even home-work, may delay the removal of staph germs from the skin. It doesn't take long for them time to reproduce and invade a scratch or an open wound.

The Centers for Disease Control (CDC) recommends frequent hand washing, showering after sports participation, and not sharing towels or other personal equipment as the first line of protection against MRSA. Even if it were staph, I could most likely help him as most strains of staph that athletes carry are not MRSA and are sensitive to most antibiotics. The real question, however, was where and when could I start on his social problem? I examined his leg and found a large red wound with red streaks running up to his groin, which was filled with firm, tender lymph nodes.

"Let's start with an antibiotic shot, and then I'll give you some pills," I explained. "Don't worry about the cost; I'll take care of that."

When I returned with the pills, Nurse Debbie had just finished his injection. He was rubbing his injured muscles while he told her, "That didn't hurt as much as getting hit by a 250-pound lineman."

Nurse Debbie left and he turned to me and asked, "Is it okay if I work tonight?"

"I thought you said you didn't work during the school year?" I asked, puzzled.

"Oh, I'm sorry," he said, "I meant that I didn't work much during school. I only work Monday nights. I help clean Joey's restaurant after they close. I really need to save some money for college."

"Dennis," I said. "I'm sorry, but you can't be on that leg tonight. I'm hoping we'll be able to get you on the field Friday night. Let me see you tomorrow after school and we'll talk more about it then. There are some other things I want to talk about, too."

I saw Dennis the next day and much to my relief, he was markedly improved.

"Hey," I almost shouted. "Looks like we got things under control and you'll be picking passes Friday night. I'll see you before the game to make a final decision."

Then I added, "How do you find the time to play football, work, and study?"

"It's not a matter of finding time," Dennis insisted. "I need to do all those things. If I don't study, I'll lose my scholarship and never get one for college. I have to work during the school year to keep my summer job. And I definitely need the money for college."

He didn't say why he needed to play football and I was afraid to ask him as I thought he might say it was the only place he could get a warm shower. He played basketball in the winter months and baseball in the spring, so I might have been right. While I was lost in thought, he continued.

"My school counselor said not to worry about getting a scholarship to college because I was black and that would give me an advantage. When he said that, I really did a dumb thing. I got mad and just walked out of his office because I think if you want something, *you need to want it bad enough to work for it*. Otherwise, it will never mean anything to you."

My eyes filled up and my throat tightened. I couldn't respond. I stood and walked over to the sink and washed my hands. I've found that's a good place to clear my mind and take a few minutes to think. As I dried my hands, I looked at Dennis and said, "Dennis, you can't imagine how proud I am to know you. Your mother must just be bursting with pride. I think you are 100 percent right. The world needs more men like you!"

"Thanks," he beamed, smiling and showing all his beautiful teeth. He interrupted that smile with a frown and said softly, "It's not easy, you know."

"I'm sure it isn't," I replied. "But like you said … if it were easy, it probably wouldn't mean much." Then I added, "I don't think you did wrong at all by leaving the counselor's office. I think you did exactly the right thing. If you had stayed there, you may have started to argue with him, and then things could have gone really bad for you. But don't you think you're maybe being a bit too hard on yourself?"

"What do you mean?" he asked, unsure if I were criticizing him.

"Well, I think the world of you and so does Coach; he and I both respect you for who you are. But you think of your situation as a weakness, while Coach and I think it has strengthened you. I wonder if you think asking for help is also a sign of weakness. You don't need to do everything yourself. Just take your leg infection as an example. If you hadn't asked for help, you would still be sick and you might have ended up losing that leg or even your life."

We talked more about his situation before Dennis left with a bit of the burden off his shoulders. He promised to talk to Coach about some of the things going on in his life. I learned that day that true character can be developed at a young age.

No Shame in Working Hard

There's a lot to be learned from Dennis. Too often we parents try to make everything easy for our kids; we don't want them to have to work too hard. It's a lesson we learned from our parents. Actually, it's a lesson we've learned from antiquity. Working hard—in the absence of compulsion—was not the norm for Hebrew, classical, or medieval cultures.[139] It was not until the Protestant Reformation that physical labor became culturally acceptable for all persons, including the wealthy. Even today we refer to the habit of work as the "Protestant Work Ethic."

We read in the Old Testament that after the fall of Adam, God said, "By the *sweat* of your brow you will eat your food…[emphasis added]." Work was seen as a curse imposed by God upon Adam and Eve and their descendants, a punishment for disobedience and ingratitude. Work was not seen as a source of joy for accomplishment or for its own intrinsic worth, only as a means to prevent poverty and destitution.

The Greeks also thought of work as a curse reserved for slaves, allowing free men to pursue warfare, large-scale commerce, and the arts—especially architecture or sculpture. Roger B. Hill from the University of Georgia notes:

> [P]hilosophers such as Plato and Aristotle made it clear that the purpose for which the majority of men labored was 'in order that the minority, the elite, might engage in pure exercises of the mind—art, philosophy, and politics (Tilgher, 1930, p. 5).[140]

I learned from Dr. Lannigan, my professor in Philosophy 101, that Aristotle thought work was a waste of time; that it interfered with man's pursuit of virtue; that knowledge for the sake of knowledge was the highest form of knowledge and that learning for the sake of earning was the lowest. (I yearned for knowledge for the sake of earning, and somehow I did not feel I stood out from the rest of the class.)

During the reformation, Martin Luther taught that work was a form of prayer; that God determines a man's profession at birth and it was sinful to try to change your birth occupation.[141] According to John Calvin's theology of predestination, not working and being idle was a sign of being damned and working hard in any occupation was a sign of being one of the Elect—those predestined for heaven.[142] These two theologians were responsible for the change in attitude toward work; we owe the term "Protestant Work Ethic" to them.

Developing a Positive Work Ethic

Dr. L. Braude in her book *Work and Workers* states that children are often influenced by others' attitudes toward work.[143]

> "If a parent demonstrates a dislike for a job or a fear of unemployment, children will tend to assimilate these attitudes. Parents who demonstrate a strong work ethic tend to impart a strong work ethic to their children."[144]

Baude's philosophy was promulgated more than thirty years ago, and it is still true today. If you want your children to have a work ethic like Dennis you must have one yourself.

Unfortunately, Dale Dauten, writing in the March 25, 2007, *Boston Globe*, says the work ethic is dead. "Younger generations in the workforce have killed it off. If you're under thirty, 'work' has a different meaning than it did." What's needed, he says, is a "way of working beyond mere work, something higher, something finer. What's needed is a Contribution Ethic." He suggests ten ways to develop a Contribution Ethic:

- Make yourself useful.
- Be a team player.
- Know your half of the workload is 60 percent.
- Expect new ideas to be met with resistance.
- Don't expect reward for everything you give.
- Assume the best in others.
- Know that being right is overrated.
- Being wrong is underrated, but leads to wisdom.
- Read.
- Think like a hero; work like an artist.

Dauten's contribution ethic will not guarantee success in the workplace, but it does mean you'll be pleased with your contribution.

Whatever your ethic—Protestant Work Ethic or Contribution Ethic—your attitude will be reflected in your kids' approach to work. As in everything else, they will emulate you. As parents, we all need to encourage our kids to work, not just so they can have a nice car or new clothing or another electronic toy, but because having things too easy can lead kids to an entitlement mentality which destroys creativity, incentive, and ambition.

When we really look at ourselves, how many of us take the easy way out instead of doing the hard, more courageous thing? When I graduated from college the commencement speaker gave each of the graduates a small pocket dictionary and a tiny penknife. Then he asked us to look up the word "expedient."

"Look at the second definition," he said. "Now take your knife and cut it out of the book, and out of your lives."

The second definition reads "based on or guided by self-interest." We did as he requested then and there. Hopefully some of us try to act accordingly.

Dennis was a senior when I left Wisconsin, so I don't know where he went to college or if he got a scholarship. I do know he made the National Honor Society and continued to do well in sports. I wouldn't be surprised to see his name in the paper someday having won accolades for some great success. And when that happens, I'll know he earned it because he wanted it bad enough to work for it.

Tool 12

Money

I don't like money, actually, but it quiets my nerves.

—Joe Lewis

Fashion, sex, drugs, and money dominate the minds of many adult as well as children and teens. This way of thinking leads many teens and their parents into heated arguments over high credit card charges and cell phone bills. The result is a growing dissatisfaction between parents and their children. Ultimately, capitalism seems to be the worst economic system in which to raise a child; at least, that's what I beginning to think until Pat came into my office providing me with a more realistic image than the one Hollywood promulgates as a means to sell movie tickets and boost ratings.

"Sorry about the way I smell," Pat began as I entered the exam room. "I just came from work and I didn't have time to go home and change," he explained. "I have a rash I want you to look at."

Pat was a plain-looking blonde kid of barely 15. His appearance that day was startling. His shorts were dirty, crumpled, and partly hidden by a tattered Braves T-shirt. And he didn't smell much better. I had seen him many times before, but only in prep shirts and pressed pants or his private school uniform—tie and all. He was from a very wealthy family, so I was a bit surprised by the way he looked and even more amazed that he had a job.

"Where do you work?" I asked.

"Peachtree Animal Hospital," he announced with pride. "You know where that is?"

"Sure, I take my dog there. What do you do?"

"I clean dog cages," he answered, betraying no emotion that showed he considered his job below his social or personal standing.

"Oh," I said surprised again. "Are you planning to be a veterinarian?"

"Not a chance."

Now I was confused. "Then why are you working in such a place?"

"Well, I need to fund my IRA, and it's the only job I could get that was close enough to walk or bike to."

That made sense. Too bad more people don't think like Pat. To encourage him I quickly added, "I'm proud of you, Pat. I guess you're never too young to get a job or start making money."

"It's not just making money that's important, you know," he pronounced, with that know-it-all-teenage-look in his eye. "Lots of people make money but still never have money."

"I'm sure that's true," I answered, not revealing whether I was one of those people he singled out. I was still a bit confused but interested enough to take the bait. "So what's important then?"

"Saving money! You see, *the best way to make money is to save money*. If you make a dollar, you really only have about 75 cents. They take the rest out for taxes and stuff. But if you save a dollar, you have a dollar. And if you invest it right, by the end of the year you should have more than a dollar; maybe a dollar five or ten or even more. It's even better if you put it into a Roth IRA, because then you get it back tax-free. You don't even have to pay taxes on the earnings!"

Pat's grin told me this was a lecture he had heard many times from adults, and he now delighted in giving it back to a grown-up. His parents would be proud.

Learning to Save

Pat is so right to urge high school kids to open Roth IRA or other suitable savings accounts. If they save $2,000 a year during their four high school years and never save another penny, and it grows tax deferred at 10% annually it will be worth just under a million dollars by the time they reach age 65.

The chart below shows how $2,000 invested each year at ages 14, 15, 16, and 17 would grow if it earned 10 percent annually tax free.

It's unbelievable to see what compounding interest really does. Of course, the future is hard to predict and annual percentage yields will vary from year to year. At this time, 10 percent yearly earnings on an investment is a highly optimistic if not impossible but, over the course of time the market has averaged more than 10% yearly growth. Who knows what the future will bring? Regardless of the growth obtained, your best choice is to invest early and consistently with focus on your long-term goals.

In contrast to investing early, a 45-year-old would have to invest just over $1,000 dollars every month, that's over $12,000 a year, until he reached 67—a total investment of $280,000—to have just over a million dollars (using a 10 percent annual rate of return). I sure wish Pat had talked to me when I was 14.

It is possible for a teen to start a Roth IRA, but it has to be with money they have actually earned.[145] According to a study by Yankelovich, a market research firm in North Carolina,[146] more than six million teens are employed. An additional million are looking for work. Teens in 2006 earned more than $480 monthly; surely they can find a way to save part or all of the $2,000 they are allowed to put into a Roth IRA.

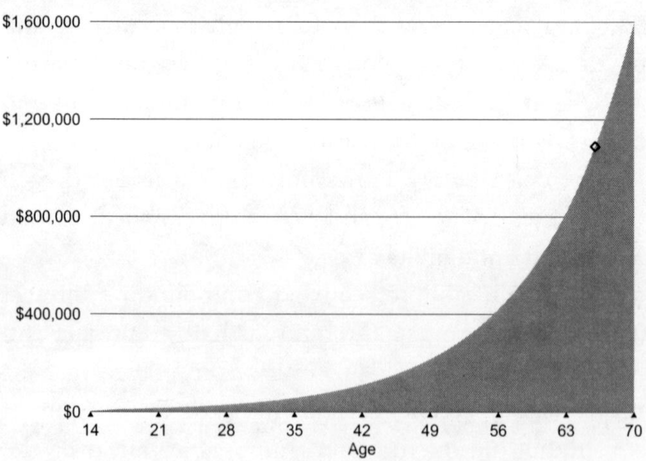

Tax deferred growth of $2,000 invested annually between ages 14 and 17 at a 10% rate of return

Critics might say that 50 years from now, a million dollars will not be worth the same as it is today. And they would be right. But it will be worth a lot more than the car a high school kid bought 50 years earlier with his $8,000. Yet high school and college kids persist in buying cars, video games, and clothes, knowing that in a few short years the car will be worth little or nothing, the game outdated, and the clothing out of style.

Getting an employed adult to save for retirement is hard enough, but talking to a teen about retirement is like trying to convince a rock to roll uphill. So if Pat is going to convince other kids to start a Roth IRA, he has his work cut out for him. Perhaps a nudge from parents will get a high schooler on his way to saving.

The Value of Work

Most neighborhoods have work available for teenagers who want to do it. When my oldest grandson was in fourth grade, his neighbor (who had three large dogs) paid him to clean the dog droppings out of his yard. Each Saturday, he made five dollars for what many would consider unpleasant work. When he was older, he began shoveling walks and mowing lawns for other neighbors. Latter he worked at a Dairy Queen; then he was a host at Applebee's; he served ice cream at a local ice cream shop, and continued his mowing jobs. He had a good grade point, a letter in cross-country track, and was field marshal in Ohio's Oakwood High School marching band. But the best financial news was that he received an ROTC scholarship which covers tuition and expenses, plus provides a stipend.This summer he graduated from college in top 5% of ROTC graduates. This accomplishment will assure him of getting one of his first picks for his first Army assignment as a second lieutenant. Hard work pays off!

While I practicing medicine in Wisconsin many years ago, a "welfare mother" brought her 12-year-old son to see me. He had hurt his leg the night before and X-rays showed a fractured tibia (the large bone in the lower leg). I asked her why she hadn't brought him in when it happened. He answered for her and said he had to deliver his papers.

"How did you manage that with a broken leg?" I asked.

"It wasn't easy," he answered. "I put my papers and my hurt leg in a coaster wagon I found in the garage and pedaled along with my good leg. It worked okay as long as I hit the front porch, but if I missed I had to hop on one leg up to the step and replace the paper. When I got done it was dark, and Mom didn't want to bother you at night."

That was more than 30 years ago, but I can still see the tears in his blue eyes.

"I wish you had called me when it happened. I would have been glad to see you, and I'm sure one of my sons would have delivered the papers for you," I assured him.

Much to his dismay, I put his leg in a cast and told him he would have to get a substitute for his route.

"How long before I can walk?" he asked.

"Let me see you in a week and if you're doing well, we can make a walker out of your cast and you'll be free. Is that soon enough?" I asked.

"I guess," he mumbled. "But I really need to do my route!"

"What are you saving for?"

"I'm not saving any of it," he answered, not trying to cover the fact. "Mom and I need it for food and stuff."

If this 12-year-old could work a paper route with a broken leg, I would think most high school kids could work and save some of their money!

Fortunately, some teens are saving money. A study by Schwab showed that in 2011, 52% of teens had a saving account with an average balance of over $900. Not such good news is that 42% had a debit card and 28% were already in debt.[147] The really bad news is, none reported that they had a Roth IRA.

Studies show that teens are a lot more like Pat than the media likes to portray. A survey of 4,400 young people (ages 12 to 19) reported in *The Cleveland Plain Dealer* showed that half "try hard" to save money. While a third usually spends most of their money, 60 percent said not being able to buy everything they wanted made them appreciate the things they were able to buy.

The average American teenager spent $107 a week in 2006. But the recession brought that number down to $20 by 2013. Moreover, 63 percent of the teens surveyed thought credit cards were dangerous, that they allowed people to spend more money than they actually had.

Fortunately, only 7 percent of teens in the 12 to 17 age group have credit cards.[148] But once they got those cards, they got into debt fast; they had an average of $1,533 in credit card debt by the time they started college and $3,262 by the time they graduated. In fact, "7% to 10% of students will drop out of college due to credit problems," says Robert Manning, author of *Credit Card Nation*.[149]

The Dangers of Debt

Once again, kids are following their parents' examples. Credit card debt in this country is sinking a lot of households under trillions of dollars of red ink. And the stress this creates is affecting family relationships. According to the Federal Reserve Board (which conducts surveys every three years), 76 percent of American households had credit cards in 2004. Of those cardholders, 55 percent paid the debt off every month and had no balance. In January 2013 those who did not pay the balance in full had an average balance of $7,122. But 10 percent of the cardholders had cumulative balances in excess of $15,000.[150]

If you have $1,000 in debt on your card and only pay the minimum, it will take you almost 15 years to pay it off at a cost of over $2,500 in interest. If you ever listen to Dave Ramsey on radio, you will know how threatening debt and its consequent interest are to a family's happiness. That interest can eat you alive! Dave Ramsey suggests you eat beans and rice until you have paid off all your credit cards,[151] but according to an article on the MSN Money Web site, there are many other ways to find the money to pay off those cards:

> Pay less to Uncle Sam. In 2011, tax-payers got an average tax refund of $3,011 and in 2012, the average fell a little to $2,946.268.5 By adjusting your withholdings, you can keep that money in your own pocket and put an extra $200- $250 a month toward your debt. (Why give the government an interest free loan?)
>
> Curb your spending. Even small changes, like brown-bagging lunch or renting one DVD a week instead of three, can free up to 10% or 15% of your income. To find expenses you can shave, track your spending for seven days. You may be surprised at how relatively small expenses—like $2.00 for a Diet Coke from the vending machine or $3.25 for a Latté—add up over time.
>
> "Control your cards. Paying down a big debt is hard enough without adding more fuel to the fire. To avoid the temptation to spend, lock your credit cards away. People have frozen them in bowls of ice or given them to a trusted friend (to use only if there is a real cash emergency). But we all agree what an emergency is, and a shoe sale at Nordstrom isn't it."[152]

It would be a good idea to include your children in the journey as you get out of debt. Experts say that parents—as with so many things in life—are the most important role models for how their teens will handle money and value it. Rob Brough, senior vice president for marketing at Zion's Bank, was quoted in *The Deseret Morning News* as saying, "If Mom and Dad don't save money and plan their spending, their kids won't be good at it either."[153] That bodes ill for today's teens. Statistics from the U.S. Bureau of Economic Analysis show Mom and Dad often are not providing a good example. Americans saved a negative 0.4 percent of their disposable personal income in the fourth quarter of 2005 and a negative 1 percent in all of 2006.[154] This means they are saving nothing and are, in fact, losing money each quarter by spending more than they earned. That is the worst rate of saving in 73 years; the only years that Americans saved less were 1932 and 1933 during the great depression. In the 1940s, Americans saved almost one-fourth of their disposable personal income and as recently as August 2004, saved 4 percent. These reported "savings" do not include what they have put away in a retirement account or have earned as a pension. But money in retirement and pension plans is not available in an emergency. Economists recommend that people have three to six months of living expenses in an emergency saving's account as we never know what the future may bring. But the good news is that in 2012 Americans saved 3.7% of their income.

Even though our schools are currently facing an overload with the classes they are required to provide, it would be great if high schools, like parents, could consider adding money-management classes to their curriculum. (Fortunately, some schools currently offer a little of this information through their Economics classes.) In the Schwab survey mention above, 86% of teens said they are interested in learning more about money, budgets, and saving. Bob Bough recommended that parents have young children sit down with them "to pay the bills for gas and electricity and the telephone. That will help them realize that all this stuff costs money."[155] He also recommended saving for things like a baseball glove or a CD. If grade-schoolers develop the habit of saving, they will be more open in high school to start saving for retirement by opening a Roth IRA. But before they do, we parents have to show them a better example.

The Joy of Giving

Starting young is important. A British survey showed that English teens had about twice as much saved before they entered their later teen years than when they entered their twenties. During these years, savings were cut in half. Cars, auto insurance, gasoline, and dating all started to absorb cash.

Helping older teens navigate the increasingly difficult adult world of finance is critical. We don't want them giving up and cashing in on the most readily available credit card like so many adults. This pattern will lead them to a lifetime of financial woes.

Money management is more than just earning, spending, and saving; it also includes giving back to the community. Every wage earner can learn the joy of giving; it is learned from parents by example and direction. Teens love to work and save and when they start donating to a favorite charity, they love that, too.

It helps them feel good about themselves; they know they are contributors and no longer living off the "fat of the land."

Once kids have established the habit of giving and realize that it truly is better to give than receive, they will usually continue it for life. A study in the March 2008 issue of *Science* magazine found that people who give to charity really are happier than those who do not. They sampled 632 adults and had them estimate their level of happiness. Then they had them estimate what percent of their income they gave to charity or gifted to friends or relatives. They found a link between giving and happiness. In order to find out which came first, they gave a small amount of money, $5 to $20, to each of 46 students. Some had to spend the money on themselves while the others had to buy a gift for someone else. Those who spent the money on others were happier than those who kept it, independent of how much money they received.[156]

Some years ago Oprah had a show called "The Big Give" I never saw the show, but reports said that watching someone else enjoy giving money away makes the viewer happy. It was reported in an article in the March 27, 2008, issue of *The Tennessean* that a Nashville woman who was on the show was not able to give away $100,000 during the week she was in Florida. She tried as hard as she could, but she ran out of time. She said, "This experience has changed my life. … It's like being baptized, because it has changed my sense of purpose. … It's like seeing life though a set of fresh eyes."

Money may not buy happiness, but giving it away apparently can!

Back to Pat. As we talked, I reemphasized that he was right about the Roth IRA and taxes: when he takes that million dollars out of his Roth IRA, it will be tax-free. He made a tough investment choice by finding a place he could walk to work (no car expense), taking a job a lot of folks wouldn't want (cleaning dog cages), and saving his earnings for the future.

I told Pat his CEO dad must be very proud of him. Then, while continuing to talk "high finance," I had a look at his leg. He had a patch of poison ivy dermatitis from a hike in the woods the previous weekend. As he left, he thanked me for the prescription and I thanked him for the lesson on finance.

While I didn't hand over my stock and banking portfolio for Pat to manage, he left me feeling good about the future and the ability of teens to cope with the materialistic world we adults have left them. We don't want our children to think that the acquisition of money is the purpose of life, but we also understand that their ability to manage money will reduce stress in their lives and in their relationships with their spouses and children. Understanding the role of finances will also permit them to donate to charity, become philanthropists, and help the less fortunate. Money does not buy happiness. But teaching our children to manage it well can reduce the kind of stress that keeps adults from taking time to smell life's roses—and being able to buy a few as well.

Parenting Tips

- Make sure at least one parent has a job at all times. If you lose your job work in a fast food restaurant or any where you can find work. Work is never demeaning.
- Your dedication to earning a living and reluctance to take a hand-out is a great teacher!
- Work hard, but don't be afraid to ask for help.
- Respect those you work for and those who work for you.
- Take your kids to work when you can. Tell them and show them what you do.
- Insist your teen finds a summer or weekend job. All work and no play may make Johnny a dull boy, but all play and no work gives him an entitlement mentality that may well doom him, as well as society.
- Save money.
- Help your kids open a savings account and make sure they save.
- Contribute to charity.
- Help your kids find a charity they can support.

Conclusion

What Does It All Mean?

> *If you really live your beliefs and make them attractive, you won't have to ram them down other people's throats—they will steal them.*
>
> —Dick Gregory

One summer noon when I was a pediatric resident, I was walking down a street in Milwaukee on my way to lunch when the light turned red. Directly in front of me was a young man with a small toddler. As we waited for the light to change, the father squatted to talk to his son. As he did so, the son also squatted. What a picture! Kids do what they see their parents do, and at every age.

It was then that I learned that kids do what we do! Plain and simple! Yes, what we say in important, but what we do is what they will do. This realization scared me! I was a young father with three sons, age 3, 4, and 5. How was I going to be a father to them! Even scarier, I would have parents ask me how to be good parents! What will I say? More importantly, what will I do?

I am sure that you have all asked yourselves these same questions. Good parents continually reappraise their parenting style. I also know that this book makes parenting look easy and while it is not a "walk in the park", a walk in the park may well be one way of making parenting easier. A walk is just one of the many times and places where you can converse with your offspring. These informal talks are an opportunity to learn what's going on inside your kids' heads.

These conversations must begin at a very early age. Many years ago while working in urgent care I saw15 year old single mother with her infant. Mom brought baby in because he had fever, vomiting, and diarrhea. After reviewing the course of the illness with Mother, I began to examine her baby. As I felt his tummy, he grimaced and I asked him it that hurt. Mother smiled. Later, during the exam he frowned when I moved his legs, Again, I asked if that hurt; and this time Mother smiled and laughed out loud.

"How is that funny?" I asked, probably letting my lack of sleep show.

"Babies can't talk." She answered.

I was quick to explain to her that she was right; babies can't talk, but babies can hear. And by hearing they learn to listen and by listening they learn to talk. That's why it's so important to talk with and read to babies!

I am often amazed that parents seem to ignore stories their kids tell them and wonder later why they don't talk when they become teenagers. Teens love to talk with each other because peers listen to them and talk with them. Too often teens and younger kids think parents are not interested in what they say or do. By giving them your undivided attention when they talk to you shows them your love and interest which has a life-long effect on their character. That's why God gave us parents, isn't it?

Country music artist Rodney Atkins in his 2007 hit song "Watching You" hits it on the head. In the lyrics, a young boy curses and when the dad asks where he learned the offensive word the boy explains that he's been watching his dad. Dad, of course feels awful and when he thinks his son is not watching he bows his head and prays for guidance in being a dad. But, his son was watching. That evening at bed time Son kneels and prays a beautiful prayer. Dad asks where he learned to pray like that. Son answers, "I've been watching you."[157]

So to paraphrase Eric from Tool 10, "Be the adult you want your child to become!"

I hope that you have enjoyed the stories in this book; through them you have been able to peer behind the sometimes closed doors of children's minds. You will find as you listen to your kids talk, watch them play, and see and hear them interact with others that they too, have wisdom like that portrayed by the kids discussed here. The operative words though are "listen, hear, watch and see". When you hear and see them you will know and always remember their stories, and they in turn will remember yours.

There is a Native American proverb that it is well to remember:

Tell me a fact and I'll learn, tell me a truth and I'll believe, but tell me a story and it will live in my heart forever.

Endnotes

1 "The State of our Nation's Youth 2005–2006," Horatio Alger Association, http://www.horatioalger.com/pdfs/state05.pdf.

2 Michael Resnick, "National Longitudinal Study of Adolescent Health," JAMA 278(10) (September 10, 1997):823–32

3 James Dobson, "What is the answer to curbing teenage sexual activity?"Focus on the Family, April 2001. Can be accessed at http://family.custhelp.com/cgi-bin/family.cfg/php/enduser/std_adp.php?p_faqid=828.

4 Lynn Minton, "Fresh Voices," Parade Magazine, August 22, 1999.

5 Tom Boyle, "St. Pius Men Hear Talk on Fatherhood," The Georgia Bulletin, February 22, 2001.

6 Traffic Safety Facts (July 2007), "2006 Traffic Safety Annual Assessment–A Preview," NHTSA, http://www-nrd.nhtsa.dot.gov/Pubs/810791.PDF; Traffic Safety Facts (updated March 2008), "Alcohol Impaired Driving," NHTSA, http://www-nrd.nhtsa.dot.gov/Pubs/810801.PDF.

7 Sylvia Slaughter, "Family sees dream home come to life," The Tennessean, August 5, 2006, Main News section.

8 Lisa Fernandez and Ben Aguirre, Jr., "Mother's sacrifice saves son from pit bull," Oakland Tribune, September 6, 2007, Media News story.

9 Myrna Weissman et al., "Remissions in Maternal Depression and Child Psychopathology," JAMA 295(12) (March 22/29, 2006):1389–98.

10 I. Akman et al., "Mothers' postpartum psychological adjustment and infantile colic," Archives of Disease of Children 91(5) (May 2006): 417–19.

11 31 Lindsey O'Connor, If Mama Ain't Happy, Ain't Nobody Happy!: Making the Choice to Rejoice, (Eugene, Oregon: Harvest House Publishers, 2006).

12 Kris and Brian Gillespie, When Mama Ain't Happy, Ain't Nobody Happy: 52 Secrets Uncovered! Rules That Women Want Men to Know (Tulsa, OK: Insight International, 2000).

13 Michael J. Formica, "Gender Differences, Sexuality and Emotional Infidelity," Psychology Today, January 8, 2009, http://www.psychologytoday.com/blog/enlightened-liv-ing/200901/gender-differences-sexuality-and-emotional-infidelity.

14 Kyle Pruett and Marsha Kline Pruett, Partnership Parenting, How Men and Women Parent Differently and How it Helps Your Kids, (Cambridge:Da Capo Lifelong Books, 2009).

15 Cal Thomas, "Hope for conservative woman president," Dispatch Politics, a division of The Columbus Dispatch, June 7, 2008.

16 Ibid

17 7 Kate Howard, "Parents can keep GPS eye on teen driver's every turn," The Tennessean, June 20, 2007, Main News Section, A1.

18 Dwight Lewis, "Know right where your teen is; it is life and death," The Tennessean, December 15, 2005.

19 Ibid.

20 John O'Sullivan, The President, the Pope, and the Prime Minister, Three Who Changed the World (Washington, DC: Regnery Publishing, Inc., 2006), 164.

21 Martha Marino and Sue Butkus, "Eat Better; Eat Together: Research on Family Meals," Washington State University, http://nutrition.wsu.edu/ebet/background.html; "For happy teens, pass the peas," The Atlanta Journal-Constitution, August 16, 1997, A7

22 The National Center on Addiction and Substance Abuse at Columbia University Annual Report, September 2007, Accompanying Statement by Joseph A. Califano, Jr., Chairman and President of the Board of Directors, "The Importance of Family Dinners IV," Sponsored by The Safeway Foundation, accessed at http

23 Op. cit., Marino and Butkus://www.casacolumbia.org/absolutenm/articlefiles/380-Importance%20of%20Family%20Din¬ners%20IV.pdf.

24 Ibid

25 Katharine Coon et al., "Relationships Between Use of Television During Meals and Children's Food Consumption Patterns," Pediatrics 107(1) (January 2001):e7.

26 J. Serpell, "Beneficial effects of pet ownership on some aspects of human health and behavior," Journal of the Royal Society of Medicine 84 (1991): 717–20.

27 "14 Ways to Show Love for Your Child This Valentine's Day," American Academy of Pediatrics, February 2009, http://www.aap.org/advocacy/releases/febvaltips.cfm.

28 Ownby et al., "Exposure to dogs and cats in the first year of life and risk of allergic sensitization at 6 to 7 years of age," JAMA 288(8) (2002): 963–72.

29 P. Cullinan et al., " Early allergen exposure, skin prick responses, and atopic wheeze at age 5 in English children: a cohort study." Thorax 59 (October 2004): 855–61; Eva Rönmark et al., "Four-year incidence of allergic sensitization among schoolchildren in a community where allergy to cat and dog dominates sensitization: Report from the obstructive lung disease in northern sweden study group," The Journal of Allergy and Clinical Immunology 112(4) (October 2004): 747–54; Sid

Kirchheimer, "Pets May Prevent Allergies in Kids," WebMD Health News,{END ITALICS http://www.webmd.com/allergies/news/20031014/pets-may-prevent-allergies-in-kids.

30 C. M. Chen et al., "Dog ownership and contact during childhood and later allergy development," European Respiratory Journal 31(5) (May 2008 [Epub Febuary 6, 2008]): 963–73.

31 Karen Allen, Jim Blascovich, and Wendy B. Mendes, "Cardiovascular Reactivity and the Presence of Pets, Friends, and Spouses: The Truth About Cats and Dogs," Psychosomatic Medicine 64 (2002):727–39.

32 Julie V. Iovine, "The healing ways of Dr. Dog," The New York Times, October 28, 2001.

33 Ibid.

34 Jeff Fisher, "Exercise has proven mental benefits, so come run to beat the blues," The Tennessean, March 28, 2008.

35 University of Tennessee College of Veterinary Medicine: a nonprofit program benefiting adolescents and dogs, "Humans & Animals Learning together," HALT, http://www.vet.utk.edu/halt/about.shtml.

36 Kris Bulcroft, "Pets in the American Family," People, Animals, Environment 8(4) (1990): 13–14.

37 Bill Strickland, "The Benefits of Pets," Parents.com, *http://www.parents.com/family-life/pets/kids/pets-good-for-kid*

James Serpell, "Guest Editor's Introduction: Animals in Children's Lives," Society and Animals, Journal of Human- even Animal Studies 7, no. 2 (1999):87–93. s/.

38 James Serpell, "Guest Editor's Introduction: Animals in Children's Lives," *Society and Animals, Journal of Human-Animal Studies* 7, no. 2 (1999):87–93.

39 Abby Deliz, "Newborns Need Touch," Suite 101. com, September 29, 2008, http://massagetherapy. suite101.com/article.cfm/newborns_need_touch.

40 A. Dougall and J. Fiske, "Surving child sexual abuse: the relevance to dental practice," Dental Update 36(5) (June 2009) 294–96, 298–300, 303–04.

41 B. M. Yarnold, "Cocaine use among Miami's public school students, 1992: religion versus peers and availability," Journal of Health and Social Policy 11(2) (1999): 69–84.

42 R. L. Poulson et al., "Alcohol consumption, strength of religious beliefs, and risky sexual behavior in college students," Journal of American College Health 46(5) (March 1998): 277–32.

43 J. M. Wallace et al., "Religion's role in promoting health and reducing risk among American youth," Health Education and Behavior 25(6) (December 1, 1998): 721–41.

44 Eric Goldscheider, "Seeking a Role for Religion on Campus," The New York Times, February 2, 2002.

45 Institute for American Values, "Hardwired to Connect: The New Scientific Case for Authoritative Communities," report by the Commission on Children at Risk, September 9, 2003, http://www.americanvalues.org/html/hardwired_press_re-lease.html.

46 Ibid.

47 Robert Shaw, M.D., The Epidemic, (New York: Regan Books, 2003): xii, 4.

48 Ibid., p. 21

49 Op. cit., Institute for American Values.

50 Amanda Aikman, "Do Children Need Religion?" Reach, September 1995.

51 Janet Daling et al., "Risk of Breast Cancer Among Young Women: Relationship to Induced Abortion," Journal of the National Cancer Institute 86(21) (1994): 1584–92.

52 Karin Michels et al., "Abortion and breast cancer risk in seven countries," Cancer Causes and Control 6:(1) (January 1995): 75–82.

53 Mads Melbye et al., "Induced Abortion and the Risk of Breast Cancer," The New England Journal of Medicine 336(2) (January 9, 1997): 81–5.

54 Karin Michels et al., "Induced and Spontaneous Abortion and Incidence of Breast Cancer Among Young Women: A Prospective Cohort Study," Archives of Internal Medicine 167 (April 2007): 814–20.

55 Abortion and breast cancer study seriously flawed, "Commentary on the Study, Michels et al. 2007," ABC, http://www.abortionbreastcancer.com/commentary/070423.

56 Joel Brind, "Induced Abortion and Breast Cancer Risk: A Critical Analysis of the Report of the Harvard Nurses Study II," Journal of American Physicians and Surgeons 12 no. 2 (2007).

57 Jesse R. Cougle et al., "Depression associated with abortion and childbirth: a long-term analysis of the NLSY cohort," Medical Science Monitor 9(4) (2003): 105–12.

58 Christian Smith with Melinda Lundquist Denton, Soul Searching, The Religious and Spiritual Lives of American Teenagers (New York: Oxford University Press, 2005).

59 Ibid., p. 216–17.

60 http://www.americanheart.org/presenter.jhtml?identifier=4422 , cited October 5, 2009.

61 Op. Cit., Smith and Demon, 154–156; 218–258.

62 Armand M. Nicholi, The New Harvard Guide to Psychiatry (Cambridge: The Belknap Press of Harvard University Press, 1988).

63 Lynn Minton, "Fresh Voices," Parade Magazine, February 14, 1999, 18.

64 T. A. Wills and S. D. Cleary, "Peer and adolescent substance use among 6th–9th graders: latent growth analyses of influence versus selection mechanisms,"

Health Psychology 18(5) (September 1999): 453–63.

65 R. W. Blum et al., Protecting Teens, Beyond Race, Income and Family Structure (Minneapolis, MN: Center for Adolescent Health, University of Minnesota, 2000)24

66 Stephen Allen, "Adolescents and Cigarette Smoking: Teens Appear to Be Using Tobacco at an Increasing Rate," Suite 101.com: The genuine article. Literally, December 8, 2008, http://substanceabuse.suite101.com/article.cfm/adolescents_and_cigarette_smoking.

67 Luther Terry, M.D., Smoking and Health, Report of the Advisory Committee to the Surgeon General of the Public Health Service (Washington, DC: U.S. Department of Health Education, and Welfare, 1964).

68 Duane Stanford, "TEEN DRIVING: Young drinkers sentenced, Gwinnett girl leaving party died in wreck," The Atlanta Journal and Constitution, November 28, 2000.

69 http://www.cdc.gov/features/alcoholconsumption/.

70 Media Center, "Ensuring Solutions to Alcohol Problems," The George Washington University Medical Center, http://www.ensuringsolutions.org/media/.

71 Ibid.

72 http://www.whitehouse.gov/sites/default/files/ondcp/newsletters/ondcp_update_june_2011.pdf.

73 Monica H. Swahn et al., "Age of Initiating Alcohol Use, Suicidal Behavior and Dating Violence Among High Risk Seventh-Grade Adolescents," Pediatrics 121 (February 2008): 297–305.

74 N. Peleg-Oren et al., "Drinking Alcohol before Age 13 and Negative Outcomes in Late Adolescence," Alcoholism: Clinical Experimental Research, 31 August 2009.

75 Sandy Fertman Ryan, "Wasted lives: the truth about teen girls and drinking," Girls' Life, Oct/Nov 2004.

76 This government study did not include 18- and 19-year-olds, perhaps partly explaining the difference from the other study. Additionally, studies have shown that fewer kids are drinking today than in 2004 when the Girls' Life article was written.

77 Office of Applied Studies, "SAMHSA's Latest National Survey on Drug Use & Health," U.S. Department of Health and Human Services, Last updated September 10, 2009, *http://www.oas.samhsa.gov/NSDUHlatest.htm*.

78 Girl Talk: Choices and Consequences of Underaged Drink-ing, "A Guide For Mothers and Daughters to Prevent Under¬age Drinking," The Century Council, www.girlsanddrinking.org.

79 Ibid.

80 Distillers Fighting Drunk Driving and Underaged Drinking, "Fight Drunk Driving," The Century Council, www.century-council.org.

81 Robert Davis, "'Hands-on' parent can keep kids off drugs," USA TODAY, February 22, 2001.

82 Op. cit., Hechinger, p. 111.

83 "How Parents Can Prevent Drug Abuse," National Crime Prevention Council, 2009, http://www.ncpc.org/topics/drug-abuse/drug-abuse/alcohol-tobacco-and-other-drugs.

84 Lisa Miller et al., "Religiosity and Substance Use and Abuse Among Adolescents in the National Survey," Journal of the American Academy of Child and Adolescent Psychiatry 39(9) (September 2000): 1190–97.

85 American Academy of Pediatrics, Committee on Public Education, "Children, Adolescents, and Television," *Pediatrics* 107(2) (February 2001):423–26.

86 "Pull the Plug,"The Tennessean, February 7, 2004.

87 Ibid.

88 Carla Kemp, "Health Briefs, Parents not following AAP TV Guidelines," AAP News, January 2004, 24:2.

89 Stephanie Strauss, "Is Media Violence Affecting Your Kids?" Nashville Parent, February 2005, 49–50. Can be viewed online at http://www.parentworld.com/news.php?viewStory=1428.

90 Daheia J. Barr-Anderson et al., "Characteristics Associated With Older Adolescents Who Have a Television in Their Bedrooms," Pediatrics 121(4) (April 2008):718–24.

91 Daheia J. Barr-Anderson et al., "Characteristics Associated With Older Adolescents Who Have a Television in Their Bedrooms," Pediatrics 121(4) (April 2008):718–24.

92 Op. cit., Kemp, p. 24, 1:2.

93 Op. cit., American Academy of Pediatrics, Committee on Public Education, p. 423–26.

94 Dimitri A. Christakis, "Can We Turn a Toxin Into a Tonic? Toward 21st-Century Television Alchemy," Pediatrics 120(3) (September 2007): 647–48.

95 Kevin Downey, "Bring the Family," Wall Street Journal, March 10, 2008.

96 Ibid.

97 "In the Matter of Violent Television Programming And Its Impact On Children," a report before the Federal Communications Commission, Washington, D.C., adopted April 6, 2007, released April 25, 2007, http://www.c-span.org/pdf/fcc_tvviolence.pdf page 14. This is an excellent article, filled with lots of well documented facts, easy to read, but a bit long. I would recommend it for anyone interested in learning more about Television's effect on children.

98 Kelli Turner, "V-chip doesn't protect kids, so TV industry now must clean up its act," The Tennessean, June 2, 2007.

99 Frederick J. Zimmerman et al., "Associations between Media Viewing and Language Development in Children Under Age 2 Years, The Journal of Pediatrics151(4) (October 2007): 364–68.

100 Ibid.

101 C. E. Landhuis et al., "Does Childhood Television Viewing Lead to Attention Problems in Adolescence? Results From a Prospective Longitudinal Study," Pediatrics 120(3) (September 2007): 532–37.

102 Dimitri Christakis et al., "Early Television Exposure and Subsequent Attentional Problems in Children," Pediat-rics113(4) (April 2004): 708–13.

103 Judith Owens et al., "Television viewing Habits and Sleep Disturbance in School Children,"Pediatrics 104(3) (September 1999): e27.

104 Op. cit., Coon, p. e7

105 Ibid.

106 Ibid.

107 Robert DuRant et al., "The Relationship Among Television Watching, Physical Activity, and Body Composition of Young Children," Pediatrics 94(4) (October 1994): 449–55.

108 M. S. Tremblay and J. D. Willms, "Is the Canadian child obesity epidemic related to physical inactivity?" International Journal of Obesity 27 (2003): 1100–05.

109 Barbara Dennison et al., "Television Viewing and Television in Bedroom Associated With Overweight Risk Among Low-Income Preschool Children," Pediatrics 109(6) (June 2002): 1028–35.

110 Pradeep P.Gidwani et al., "Television Viewing and Initiation of Smoking Among Youth," Pediatrics 110(3) (September 2002): 505–08.

111 Op. cit., American Academy of Pediatrics, Committee on Public Education, p. 423–26.

112 Erica Weintraub Austin et al., "The Role of Interpretation Processes and Parental Discussion in the Media's Effects on Adolescents' Use of Alcohol" Pediatrics 105(2) (February 2000): 343–49.

113 Rebecca Collins et al., "Watching sex on television predicts adolescent initiation of sexual behavior," Pediatrics 114(3) (September 2004): e280–289.

114 Diana M. Zuckerman and Barry S. Zuckerman, "Television's Impact on Children," Pediatrics 75(2) (February 1985): 233–40.

115 Kenneth Gadow and Joyce Sprafkin, "Field Experiments of Television Violence with Children: Evidence for an Environmental Hazard?" Pediatrics 83(3) (March 1989): 399–405.

116 D.A. Christakis "The Effects of Infant Media Usage: What Do We Know and What Should We Learn?" Acta Paediatr. 2009 Jan;98(1):8–16.

117 David Kleeman, The Good Things About Television http://www.media-awareness.ca/english/parents/television/good_things_tv.cfm cited October 15, 2009.

118 Op. cit., American Academy of Pediatrics, Committee on Public Education, p. 423–26.

119 Horatio Alger Study of Our Nations Youth (2005), "Teens Willing to Work Harder and Expect More From Education," Horatio Alger Association, http://www.horatioalger.com/news/05sony.cfm.

120 Op. cit., Christakis, "Early Television Exposure and Subsequent Attentional Problems in Children."

121 Ibid.

122 Heidi Aase and Terje Savolden, "Infrequent, but not frequent, reinforcers produce more variable responding and deficient sustained attention in young children with attention-deficit/hyperactivity disorder (ADHD)," The Journal of Child Psychology and Psychiatry 47(5) (May 2006): 457–71.

123 Carla Kemp, "Survey ranks top 5 drugs for children based on spending," AAP News December 2007, 28:12:2.

124 Richard M. Scheffler et al., "Positive Association Between Attention-Deficit/Hyperactivity Disorder Medication Use and Academic Achievement

During Elementary School," Pediatrics 123(5) (May 2009): 1273–79.

125 C. S. Lewis, The Screwtape Letters (New York: Harper Col-lins, 1942, renewed 1996): 50.

126 Jack Nicklaus, Golf My Way (New York: Simon & Shuster, 1972).

127 Tom Rath and Donald Clifton, How Full Is Your Bucket? (New York: Gallop Press, 2004), 28.

128 Jim Myers, "Look on the sunny side, and children will follow," The Tennessean, September 9, 2005, p. D-1.

129 Ian Newby-Clark, "Five Things You Need to Know About Effective Habit Change," Zenhabits, http://zenhabits.net/2007/11/five-things-you-need-to-know-about-effective-habit-change/.

130 Op. cit., Rath, p. 24.

131 John Locke, Some Thoughts Concerning Education, Vol. XXXVII, Part 1, The Harvard Classics (New York: P.F. Colier & Son, 1909–14; Bartleby.com, 2001), 160.

132 Elisabeth Kübler-Ross, On Death and Dying (New York: Scribner Classics, 1997).

133 "How to play target golf," Golf Digest Woman, April 2001, 99–100.

134 "Abraham Lincoln Quotes," BrainyQuote, http://www.brainyquote.com/quotes/keywords/happy.html

135 Patrick R. Steffen and Kevin S. Masters, "Does compassion mediate the intrinsic religion-health relationship?" Annals of Behavioral Medicine 30(3) (2005): 217–24.

136 Linda Kaplan Thaler and Robin Koval, The Power of Nice, How to Conquer the Business World with Kindness (New York: Currency/Doubleday, 2006).

137 Patricia Kitchen quoting Maggie Mistal, "Niceness works: A little kindness can make workplace better," Los Angeles Times-Washington Post, January 21, 2007.

138 Op. cit., Thaler and Koval, p. 3.

139 M. Rose, Reworking the work ethic: Economic values and socio-cultural politics (London: Schocken, 1985).

140 Roger B. Hill, "Attitudes Toward Work During the Classical Period," History of Work Ethic, http://www.coe.uga.edu/workethic/hatcp.html.

141 Roger B. Hill, "Protestantism and the Protestant Ethic," History of Work Ethic, http://www.coe.uga.edu/workethic/hpro.html.

142 Ibid.

143 L. Braude, Work and workers (New York: Praeger, 1975).

144 Roger B. Hill, "Influences Shaping the Contemporary Work Ethic," History of Work Ethic, http://www.coe.uga.edu/~rhill/workethic/hist.htm.

145 "Roth IRA For Teenagers," Frugaldad.com, http://frugal-dad.com/2009/01/27/roth-ira-for-teenagers/.

146 Alison Wellner, "Teens view jobs as first step to wealth," USA Weekend, June 10, 2007.

147 http://www.aboutschwab.com/images/press/teensmoneyfactsheet.pdf. Cited March 10, 2013.

148 NAA Business Analysis & Research Department: Newspaper Association of America (August 2007 p. 10), "Targeting Teens," Consumer Insight, http://www.naa.org/docs/Re-search/TargetingTeensBrief.pdf.

149 Robert D. Manning, Credit Card Nation: The Consequences of America's Addiction to Credit (New York: Basic Books, 1st Ed., 2001).

150 *http://www.nerdwallet.com/blog/credit-card-data/average-credit-card-debt-household/*. Cited March 10, 2013.

151 The Early Show, "Dave Ramsey, Money Answer Man," CBS News.com, http://www.cbsnews.com/stories/2007/01/30/earlyshow/living/money/main2413314.shtml.

152 Melody Warnick, "The Basics: Your credit card payment just doubled," MSN.Money, *http://moneycentral.msn.com/content/Banking/creditcardsmarts/P117014.asp*.

153 Carma Wadley quoting Rob Brough, "Bank on it: It pays to teach kids about money management," Deseret New Associated Press (February 1,

2007), "Personal savings drop to a 73-year low: Development comes as 78 million boomers nearing retirement," MSNBC, http://www.msnbc.msn.com/id/16922582.s, February 6, 2005, Life section.

154 Associated Press (February 1, 2007), "Personal savings drop to a 73-year low: Development comes as 78 million boomers nearing retirement," MSNBC, http://www.msnbc.msn.com/id/16922582.

155 Op. cit., Wadley.

156 Elizabeth W. Dunn et al., "Spending money on others promotes happiness," Science 319(5870) (21 March 2008): 1687–88.

157 Rodney Atkins Lyrics, "Watching You," *www.azlyrics.com*

Index